BLO
GOLI

Other books by the same author

*Inner Peace: A Source of Chinese
Philosophic Meditative Practice*

*The Eye Over the Golden Sands:
The Memoirs of a Penang Family*

LIM KEAN SIEW

BLOOD ON THE GOLDEN SANDS

The Memoirs of a Penang Family

Pelanduk
Publications
www.pelanduk.com

Published by
Pelanduk Publications (M) Sdn Bhd
(Co. No. 113307-W)
12 Lorong SS13/3E
Subang Jaya Industrial Estate
47500 Subang Jaya
Selangor Darul Ehsan, Malaysia

Address all correspondence to
Pelanduk Publications (M) Sdn Bhd
P.O. Box 8265, 46785 Kelana Jaya
Selangor Darul Ehsan, Malaysia

Cheack out our website at *www.pelanduk.com*
e-mail: *mypp@tm.net.my*

Copyright © 1999 Lim Kean Siew
Design © 1999 Pelanduk Publications (M) Sdn Bhd
All rights reserved. No part of this book may be reproduced in any
form or by any means without prior permission from the Publisher.

Perpustakaan Negara Malaysia   Cataloguing-in-Publication Data

Lim, Kean Siew, 1922-
   Blood on the golden sands / Lim Kean Siew.
   ISBN 967-978-644-7
   1. World War, 1939-1945—Pulau Pinang. 2. World War,
   1939-1945—Social aspects—Pulau Pinang. I. Title.
   959.5

Printed in Malaysia by
Swan Printing Sdn Bhd

ACKNOWLEDGEMENTS

MANY friends were instrumental in the writing of this book, especially those who lived through World War II, which has no doubt made a lasting impression on their outlook. Reliving the past with me must have been hell and I wish to thank them and to apologise for any uncomfortable feelings I must have dredged from the deep recesses of their memory.

I would also like to apologise to those whom I have mentioned in the book for any pain I might have caused as no intention of hurt was meant.

I particularly wish to thank Keith Currie, a friend of long standing, who has lived in these parts since graduating from Cambridge, and Khoo Heng Choon, for spending so much of their time proofreading my writing.

THE MANY FACES OF WAR

War has many faces, and phases,
It comes with killing, rape and torture,
Purges, ethnic cleansing, gas chambers,
The sacking of cities, wanton destruction
Of cultures and civilisations.

In the name of religion, justice,
Ideology, righteous indignation,
People are enslaved and evil brought.

Yet, from its deaths come new life,
From its pillage and destruction,
Come new cities and civilisations.

It is a paradox of many things.
To victors, red is the colour of courage,
White, the purity of mind and soul;
To the conquered, red is the colour of blood,
And white that of the shrouds of death.

In our own mirrors we see noble men;
But what do others in the same mirrors see?

I saw one of them that Singapore night,
A symbol of death in silver, tinsel bright,
Pinned by searchlights against the black sky,
Like a white tree angel on a Christmas night.

It came like an angelic being of beauty,
But in stealth and with guilty death.

Now, they glide brazenly into the dawn,
Silver grey wings glowing with red suns,
Turning white the pure blue sky
Like gulls returning from the sea.

But they have come, not for shelter
From cruel winds wracking the seas.
They have come to bring the thunder of fire
The rain of shrapnel, to bring
To an innocent childlike island
Corruption, perversion and death.

They were destined to humble
The proud Imperial nations of the West
Help usher in a new era of emancipation,
Yet they had not thought even to spare
The most innocuous of islands
Nor the innocent children there
Who had known no more than the sounds
Of the monsoon winds, its storms and surf.

I thought they looked so pretty—
Till the bombs came screaming down
To turn red the golden sands.

They came brazenly with claims,
Propaganda leaflets floating down,
With claims to set the people free,
Bold red sun emblazoning their silver wings.
Symbols, they claimed of boldness and purity,
Their wings in noble silver white.
But their leaflets floated down
With bombs to make red the golden sands.

Was Perry to blame for forcing open
The doors of Japan and letting loose
The samurai hounds of wrath who would

One day seek to humble the West
With vengeful sword and change the face
Of Asia and awaken a sleeping dragon?
The colour of the Pacific sky was blue,
The colour of its peaceful sun white,
The colour of the innocent sand was gold,
But the silver wings of their planes
Dirtied the blue sky, their red suns
Blotted out the white sun and their bombs
Turned the seas incarnadine.

In a war, the weak is shown no mercy
Nor are the innocent, nor the proud spared.
The truth is that there are none, such
As the noble or the knave, but only those
Who fight and survive to become the heroes
Or those who refuse or who fumble
Those who may not want to fight and survive
Who are called the cowards or knaves.

One must either kill or be killed
And be honoured and forgotten,
For such is the nature of war.

Don't sound the trumpets,
The dead cannot hear
The victors are too drunk
And the maimed and injured
Find the sounds too painful.

The voices you hear are not
The sounds of applause but cries
Of pain, the whimperings of pleas
Turned to the curses of the dying.

So, don't blow the trumpets or
Trample on the bleeding roses.

Even in the bold front of war, we often
See the irony, the puny man of history.
The conscript, the mercenary, the eunuch,
The flatterer concerned with himself,
Doing the killing, ignorant of the issues,
Who thinks himself great but is
Nothing but a caricature after all.

But they are not the only faces we see.
We also see the faces of those
With no concern with the war
Over whom wars are fought. Those
Tossed about by the storms of war,
The innocent who suffer in silence
The unimportant whom history will ignore.

Even as the sounds of war subside
To the silence of death, the sounds
Of the whimpering take their place
As those still alive try to shake off
The dust of the ruins and the smell
Of a past civilisation shattered,
To retread, with little more than
The slim sinews of hope, a new life
And with unsure and trembling hands,
Rebuild for themselves new homes.

For the living cannot hope to avoid
The future or look back at the dead.
Life continues and nature dictates
That their bridge to the future
Must be found where new leaders
With new promises of hope abound.

What is war but pillage and rape, and
The lowly musty smell of sweat and fear?
Who understands, even amongst the victors,

War's noble motives and high ideals
Who have fought to kill and die?

Hard, hard, hard are victorious eyes
As they burn with cold, cold gaze
Into the glazed eyes of the tortured.

Hard, hard, hard are the faces that
Gaze, eyeball to eyeball, upon
The cold glazed eyes of the dead.

Blood, blood everywhere,
And not a tiny drop is theirs.

Don't sound the trumpets,
The dead cannot hear,
The victors are too drunk,
And the maimed and injured
Find the sounds too painful.

The victorious are full of dictates,
The defeated can only whimper,
The damned are muted, bereft of curses,
Choked with the awareness of death.

Don't sound the trumpets,
Nor trample on those bleeding roses.
War is a tragicomedy that comes
At any time, in any place,
With many masks and faces
And masquerades in many graces.

War challenges the norms,
Flaunts the established,
Turns loyalties around
And makes heroes out of clowns;
Whilst the lowly mock the mighty

And fools dream lofty dreams,
Masquerading with many graces
With many masks and faces.
War can be a tragicomedy
And whilst the actors strut about,
Play little masquerades with masks
To mock the brooding adversity,
The slaughter marches on behind
The clownish gestures and graces.

Even as the world shuts its eyes in shame
To see rivers run with blood and
The very earth stained a scarlet red,
Some still search the wind and the sky
To see if the world still sings.

And, in the middle of the night,
We try to turn nightmares into sweet dreams
As we wait in hope to see the sun
Nudge the dark night and dawn's banners
Slap to life fading hope itself.

For even in the gloomiest times,
Flames still burn in kindred souls
That can spark and rekindle
The humanity within our hearts
As do earth's eternal fires
Bring back from beneath cold winter's
Crust of ice, the rites of spring
And the warmth of summer which even
Cold late frosts of winter cannot kill.

Let us not confront the winter winds
Or show our hearts in our faces
But let us cover up, keep the warmth
Within our souls with patience and wait.

And do not let the cold hard blade
Of winter's hug chill your breath

Or the cold hard blades of frost
Cut off the hidden buds of spring.
We cannot plan for everything in war
The unexpected happens. A carbuncle,
War emits poisons and must erupt
To emit poisons before it kills itself.
Pantomimes and ephemeral dreams
Of little meaning, come with treachery
And wild deliriums of grandeur,
To leave behind worthless, crippled things.

In war it is God who disposes.
We can only plan, propose and hope
To survive the unexpected. A carbuncle,
War must discharge deluding poisons,
Produce delirious pantomimes of grandeur
Fabricate wild dreams of nonsense,
To leave behind worthless, crippled things.

As we sometimes sit and watch
How the tiniest ripples can pervert
The truth by distorting the images
On the sea's surface, we also wonder
If we do not, by our emotions,
The truth distorts; provoking
The many grotesque faces of war.

Then, when the emotional winds die down
And our thoughts are stilled, we wonder
If we have not, to make grandiose our egos
And to satisfy the urges of our vanity,
Greed and ambition, used justice and beliefs
And religions as excuses to justify
The butchery of war and strife.

God works in mysterious ways.
Even as the end draws near

And our breasts begin to swell
With hope and the insanity,
The nightmares and the dreams
Draw to a close, all we can see is
Blood on the golden sands.

Where the golden grass will grow
The red poppies will also grow.
From the mud comes the lotus,
With deaths come new births.

Even when deep hatred runs the heart,
Love does not really die but hides
In the deep warmth of the soul to return
Like the faithful golden orioles in spring.

Now, sound the trumpets,
Let the bugles blow,
Instead of salutes, let them
Dig trenches, plant roses,
Grace the ponds with lotus flowers.

But don't trample the flowers
Nor tread on the tender lilies,
The flowers for the dead. Cover
Those pain-wracked faces now at peace
And bury the coffins. Then hope
That war will find another place.

Then, in the midst of this silence,
I thought I saw the Eye looking down
And a voice whispered from the sky—
"And what have you learnt from the war?"

I have learnt simple things.
That man is neither good nor bad
But is the result of his nature.

*For in him lie contradictions
Of opposites, of the good and bad,
Of greed and fear which cause
Selfishness and cowardice and
Acts of viciousness, cruelty and sadism;
Courage and generosity
That bring nobility and kindness;
And such other opposites that make up
His nature, personality and character.*

*It is dependent on which predominate
That makes him good or bad. Some
Are born to goodness, some to evil made.
They do what their nature makes them do.*

*For the welfare of all, he must
By discipline and law be controlled.*

*I now know that war comes when ambition,
And overbearing arrogance and righteousness
Dismiss the balance that make for sanity
And poke a finger into the face of law.*

*Rationalisation and self-aggrandisement
Become the rule and justification,
The excuses for murder and rape.*

*In the name of their beliefs,
They justify their acts of cruelty
As the punishment of evil and
Destruction as acts of holy sacrifice.
Self-righteousness makes the betrayals
Of friends honourable things and
Selfishness, bigotry, vanity and greed
The natural acts of human beings.
I have heard of the deeds of Genghis Khan,
Of Tamerlane the Great; of the deeds*

Of great men of history such as Alexander,
Of Napoleon and of Hitler,
Who have tried to make great nations
After their own image to last forever.

I have also heard of men who built
Great cities like Samarkand and Constantinople,
Edifices such as the Taj Mahal,
Material monuments of great and wondrous beauty
That have died or lie dying in the sun.

Men in history have done great acts
But I now know they did what they did,
Not because they believed but because
Their ambitious natures told them so.

Thus have they also distorted the truth,
Blinded themselves in their own beliefs,
Committed the most heinous of crimes as well,
Because their very natures have compelled it so.

So I think no more of greatness
Or to build such magnificence as
Flatter the ego of men or add to
Vainness and the pomp and ceremony of men;
But in more noble and cultural things
That will ennoble the human mind,
Enrich our cultures and make us turn from war.

So also have I dreamt of enrichment
Without war and in peace, wherein
I still can see such as the mighty caravans
Of ancient Samarkand plod the silk road,
Arab seafarers and Ming vessels
Traverse the seas to enrich
The cultures of different nations.

I also dream great dreams of hope,
Have visions of the mighty fortresses of faith
Where men speak in modesty and gentleness
And extend to others what he extends to himself.

I can see there is no continental divide
But an East and a West blessed as one,
Not in fear by isolation bred.

In that world I can also see such men
Of such nature as would incline to goodness.
But as nations do mirror the nature of leaders,
It becomes a danger when evil men rule
Or when their sanity is disturbed
As the elements of evil outbalance their opposites.

So, as with nations, shall it be with men.
If we are to stop the hideous cycles
Of war and peace, there shall be such
International institutions as the ill-fated League
Or the creaky United Nations but with laws
Such as are beyond the will of individual nations
And their recalcitrant leaders.

And in my dreams I still see the mountains
Where still the aspen trees grow
And there are clean lichen and mosses
Amidst the creeks and mountain springs.

I know that it is a dream I see.
But then, what distinguishes a man
But his faith and hope and his dreams.
Let us search for those springs.
For, we must not forget that beauty grows
Not only from the mud and filth,
But also in innocence and virgin lands.

CONTENTS

Acknowledgements
Preface
Prologue

1. Death of the Innocents   35
2. I Thought They Looked So Pretty   43
3. Myths and Hypocrisies   47
4. The Evacuation   53
5. Raise the White Flag   59
6. The Nature of War   69
7. The Voices You Hear   73
8. Puny Man of History   79
9. Whom History Will Ignore   85
10. In Dazed Wonderment   91
11. The Sinews of Hope   97
12. Whimpering Faces   103
13. Hard are the Faces   111
14. Not a Tiny Drop is Theirs   127
15. Don't Sound the Trumpets   137
16. Many Masks and Faces   145
17. A Tragicomedy   157
18. The World Shuts Its Eyes   165
19. Winter Cannot Kill   179
20. The Eposho   191
21. War's a Carbuncle   203
22. That We May Survive   211
23. The Truths Distort   225
24. Urges of Our Vanity   231
25. God Works in Mysterious Ways   239
26. Like the Golden Orioles in Spring   247

27. Sound the Trumpets   259
28. Electra Speaks   267

   Epilogue   273

War has many faces, and phases,
It comes with killing, rape and torture,
Purges, ethnic cleansing, gas chambers,
The sacking of cities, wanton destruction
Of cultures and civilisations.

In the name of religion, justice,
Ideology, righteous indignation,
People are enslaved and evil brought.

Yet, from its deaths come new life,
From its pillage and destruction
Come new cities and civilisations.

It is a paradox of many things.
To victors, red is the colour of courage,
White, the purity of mind and soul;
To the conquered, red is the colour of blood,
And white that of the shrouds of death.

In our own mirrors we see ourselves noble men;
But what do others in the same mirrors see?

PREFACE

PENANG was taken over by the British from Thailand in 1786, and Singapore was carved out of Southeast Asia by the Treaty of Amboyna in 1824, to become colonies during the heyday of the British Empire. Ever since then they had lived under *Pax Britannica* and had known no war.

So, when the militarists of Japan launched a total war, hoping to swallow for herself the entire region of Southeast Asia in 1941, Japan had also struck out at people who were innocent. For, though we had read of and seen war in China and Europe, it was a picture-book war without the smell and sweat of fear nor the salty taste of blood. And because of this, when Japan struck at us, the shock was all the more profound. As colonial subjects, we were not encouraged to understand politics and therefore did not quite comprehend the whys and wherefores of war; when the war came and we were hit, it was as if a whole new world had opened right before our eyes.

This is a story of what happened when a war came to Southeast Asia and hit at the British colonies of Penang and Singapore, particularly Penang, a jewel set in a tropical sea of politically childlike people whose sin was not that they wanted a war which was not of their making but because they happened to be standing in the way.

This is a story of what happened and how the people grew up in the war. Let it not be mistaken that because I had chosen to place the background of the events in Penang that it is no more than a pitiful story of a small group of people because what happened in Penang also happened in Singapore and it is a microcosm from which the macrocosm can be discerned.

I come from that little island, so I know it well. Many from the island have achieved great fame and I have described what life there was like before the war in *The Eye Over the Golden Sands*. This book is a continuation and takes in the events of the Japanese Occupation and the seeds of the growth of nationalism that was to come to the entire region after the war.

When Japan dropped its first bombs in the Pacific, it took us by surprise, but it should not have been so with the authorities who ought to have known better, for we had been assured again and again that Japan did not have the courage or the wherewithal to take on the Western powers and we had in our naivety believed that propaganda.

I was then a student in Raffles College in Singapore where almost the entire crop of post-war leaders of Malaya and Singapore of my generation was. It was in the early hours of the morning when the Japanese bombers came. It was at the same time her bombers launched their strike on Pearl Harbour.

It was in the very early hours of the morning when the Japanese bombers came. It was at the same time her bombers launched their strike on Pearl Harbour. It was to open our eyes to the lies which we had been fed for we were to be the future leaders of the region even though not all of us succeeded in our cause.

I was then housed in our college hostel for third-year students on Emerald Hill. It was not that I was a third-year student that I was there. I had been "sent down" from residence because of an incident in college where I had wrongfully slapped a waiter for rudeness. I should not have done what I did. I was one of three students, two Chinese and a Malay, who had gone out for a bicycle ride and had returned just when the dining room was closing for lunch.

We were a little late and it was up to the kitchen whether to stretch the time or refuse to give us lunch. The kitchen decided to serve us but when the soup came we found that Daud (not his real name) was served what appeared to be no more than two slices of potato in hot water.

It was none of my business. I should have let him do his bit and protest. I should have minded my business. But Daud was taken aback. He was not aggressive. All he did was to point out to us what the kitchen had done to him. But his hurt was obvious and he seemed to be saying that he had been discriminated against because he was Malay.

I called out to the waiter. He was Chinese. He refused to come out of the kitchen. I went to the door of the kitchen and he came out. I led him to our table and pointed out to him what the kitchen had done. He was surly. There was no reason why the soup could not have been thinned down in the pot before serving.

I had the strong feeling that there had been discrimination because there was resentment that we were late and he had thought to take it out on Daud. At the thought, I grew angry suddenly and before I realised it I had given him a tight slap.

I suppose I was in the wrong, but then so was he. The matter was brought up to the Master of the college. The waiter claimed I had struck him so hard that I had broken two of his teeth. That, of course, was unlikely. But what annoyed me was that I was accused by the Master of not knowing how to treat servants. I suppose that was the prerogative of the British colonials.

I pointed out quietly that I had two servants to myself in the house. It was an exaggeration, we had only three in all, but I had made my point. Nevertheless, it did not get me anywhere. I could not have been sent down from college because, in a way, though I interfered, it was on behalf of someone who had been discriminated against. Though Daud kept quiet and out of the way, nevertheless he had been wronged. So, I was sent down "from residence" instead. I had done what I thought was my duty but without thanks. After the war, we joined the Independence movement, only to play second fiddle to the Malays. Malaya belonged rightly to the Malays and though they accepted a common struggle, it was not on the understanding of equality of political power. That is a glimpse of my world before the war.

The planes came when many of my friends were fast asleep and even as I was burning the midnight oil for our term examinations that were coming the next morning. They came in stealth even as the last British soldiers were still downing their last beers. It was only after the bombs had fallen that the defences of Singapore woke up and the sirens began to sing. As the searchlights came on, my friends began to join me in the garden outside the hostel.

"What's happening?" a sleepy voice intoned behind me as we watched the last plane disappear into the night sky. It was the voice of Fred Arulanandom, who was to end his life as a Supreme Court Judge after the independence of Malaya.

"The heavens have opened," came an equally laconic reply as Morris Barker joined our small group. Then someone yawned as we watched the searchlights sweep the heavens in vain even as the engines of the planes were fast growing soft in the night sky. The bombing had awoken us from our sleep and we began slowly to crawl back into the hostel. It was to turn our world upside down.

In the college grounds the next morning, many of our college friends were gathered. The term exams were due to start that morning but as time passed, nothing seemed to be happening.

The heavens had indeed opened and so had the eyes of many of us such as Tun Abdul Razak, Ungku Aziz, Raja Badiozaman, Rajah Azam, Lee Kuan Yew, Toh Chin Chye, Goh Keng Swee (who had recently joined the teaching staff), Morris Barker and Eddie Barker, who would become politicians during the independence movement and into Independence itself. They were asking how the Japanese planes could have come so far across the sea to hit at Singapore.

There were also others such as Tuanku Jaafar (Malaysia's present King and the son of the first King), Tun Dato' Seri Dr Haji Hamdan Sheik Tahir, the Governor of Penang, and Rajah Azam Shah, the grandson of Rajah Hilir, who was said to have assassinated J.W.W. Birch as a consequence of which he was to lose his chance to become the Sultan of Perak, who were discussing their plans for they were mostly state scholars. There were also Robert Kuok, Lim Chin Khuan, Chin Fung Kee and others who would not be politicians but post-war luminaries and leaders of the Malayan and Singapore communities.

But I wonder if I could say the same thing of the British High Command in whom we had put so much trust and who had demanded so much of our loyalty. I wonder if they ever opened their eyes to the reality and the trust the people had in them. The communiqué that was to be issued on December 9, 1941, two days later had this to say: "Air reconnaissance yesterday established that twenty-five further transports were proceeding down the coast of Southern Thailand escorted by warships, apparently preparing to land additional troops in Singora, Patani and Kota Bahru. Thus all the transports that were located in the air reconnaissance of December the 6th and 7th are now apparently engaged in these landings in the Kra Isthmus and in the Northeast Malaya ..."

Indeed, if it was known that the transports were coming towards Malaya on December 6 and 7 and that Japan was on the warpath, there was no reason why the defences should have been caught by surprise that night. The planes had come even as the last military revellers were downing their last beers and returning to barracks. Only after the bombs had struck and the planes were flying off that the air raid sirens began to sound the alarm to be followed almost immediately with the all clear.

Even as we ran out to the front garden of our hostel at Mount Faber after the bombs had fallen, we could see the searchlights come on only as the planes, their engines no longer desynchronised, were on their way out of the Singapore skies and the bombs had fallen.

A silver shape caught by a searchlight which lit it up like a tiny cigar was the last plane out. When the other searchlights began to converge on it to seemingly pin it against the backdrop of the sky, it was already flying into the horizon and I could not help having a sneaking admiration for it because it seemed unperturbed by the puffs of cotton wool that seemed to explode behind it as it quietly went on its way like a pretty white tinsel angel on a Christmas tree. But it was not an angel of mercy, but a harbinger of the terror that was to fall over Malaya and Singapore.

As it slowly flew into the distance unharmed and the searchlight crews turned off their lights one by one, I thought I could sense their extreme frustration. Yes, the defences of Singapore were caught by surprise and they should not have been. In fact, with so many generals and brass in Singapore, and with an air marshal, it was a shame that there was no effective defence system then or later as the Japanese swept down the peninsula to take Singapore. Despite everything that has been written, I could not see nor feel any strong reaction of the defences against the Japanese advance. As far as I was concerned, the Indian army at the Jitra Line just collapsed as did most of the defence lines later thrown up to impede the Japanese advance.

Then came a joint CIC statement issued in Singapore the day after the bombing: "Japan's action today gives the signal for the Empire's naval, army and air forces and for the forces of its Allies to go into sanction with common aims and common ideals. We are ready; we have plenty of warning and our preparations are made. ... We are confident. Our defences are strong and our weapons efficient ..."

Yet, within the first week of the war, the air force had been negated and the country had been laid bare of its defences. Who was responsible for this, our incompetence, complacency or Japan's capabilities? Or was it true that we were being fed with platitudes and that Britain was too concerned with fighting for her own life to be concerned with a colony so many miles away? Indeed, our eyes had been opened and we had seen. If the eyes of the defence chiefs had been opened, they did not seem to have seen what was coming.

The heavens, indeed, had opened for us. From a languid, lazy and lackadaisical world, we were catapulted into a world of somersaults and frenzy from which we would never recover.

PROLOGUE

MANY people wonder why Japan went to war in 1941. It is difficult to answer this question because there are many causes and reasons for war nor would I attempt it but by way of an introduction to this book because this book is concerned with this war and how it affected us.

But to understand my point of view, it is necessary that my synopsis of the history that war has brought is given. But I will provide no more than a brief synopsis to bring out what I wish to say and not a long diatribe because a wordy one with historical details could distract, confound and obscure the main issues, just as one can see the beautiful silhouette of our mountains and skyline at dusk or dawn before the details cloud and confuse them and we would miss the wood for the trees, so to speak.

Japan practised a feudalistic social structure with a shogunate, inspired by the warlord system of ancient China, and developed by a *bushido* culture into a *samurai* civilisation despite its Buddhist influence. There had been successful Roman Catholic Portuguese incursions into the country, but when Commodore Perry forced open her doors, their inability to resist America, brought about a shock. Perry did not realise that he had, by forcibly opening the doors of Japan, also unleashed upon the world an aggressive Japanese spirit.

It is not easy to understand what happened without an understanding of the culture and structure of Japanese society. I say this because racism itself is not the only reason for enmity between people and states. It is the state of the national mind, the culture and the social thinking which go to make up racism and national identities that are the underlying causes. That is why ethnic differences have a better meaning than race as a person of a race can change under the influence of another culture. Buddhism, operating within a shogunate structure imbued with the *bushido* spirit as manifested in the *samurai*, was Zen. In that way she was a different flock from the other Buddhist countries of Asia.

Instead of doing the expected, after Perry, Japan examined herself to understand why she was not powerful enough to resist the West. She did not change her structure or her thinking except that she quickly and determinedly modernised her military and rearmed herself to match power with power.

The chance to prove herself came just after the turn of the century when she sank the Russian Far East fleet. She had flexed her muscles and the West was silent, so she annexed Korea which called herself the Land of the Morning Calm. Surprised at the disinterest of the West and with the excuse that she needed land for her overcrowded cities, she continued and turned Manchuria into a puppet land. Then she began her quest to turn China into a colony.

We have to admit that it was strange that Marshal Yuen Shih Kai should have kidnapped Chiang Kai Shek to compel him to declare war on Japan unless we understand why Japan should have been aggressive whilst the rest of Asia was placid and weak against foreign aggression even if they were full of internal strife and feuds.

If I have to give a reason, I would say it was because of misapplied Buddhism which allowed pacifism as an excuse for cowardice. The Asian countries were Buddhist and it was not by chance alone that armed resistance came through the secular Communist front forces of those countries.

In Annam, or Cambodia, Laos and Vietnam, and in China, it was the Communist forces that provided the inspiration and the backbone of resistance against the Japanese and the other foreign powers. Why? Precisely because they were secular and not riven by superstitions and the pacifism of Buddhism.

China did fight. But it was not the Nationalists who were in the spiritual forefront of the war. Chiang Kai Shek had to be coerced by the young Marshal Yuan whilst the Communist armies under Mao needed no such persuasion.

But Japan was also Buddhist. Why was she different? Buddhism taught *samatha* and *vipassanna* meditation. One tradition of meditation in China which was to influence Japan was the *samatha* technique known as the Chen technique. This was to become the Zen, a characteristic of which was the one-pointed or single-minded concentration technique.

But Japan married this to the Shogunate tradition instead of to the Tao and its superstitions so that its single-mindedness went into the culture of the warrior class of Japan, making its single-mindedness of purpose even stronger, not necessarily for peace.

In their martial arts, for example, the trainee is taught, again and again, to concentrate on a point of weakness of the enemy in order to dispose of him by attack at his weakest point. Those who practised with the stick learnt to disable their opponents with one solid blow, preferably right on the top of his head and he practised it to perfection. Those who practised the art with a sword, practised to demolish their opponents with a single stroke of the sword. And they learnt all this with complete single-mindedness and performed it on command. They were trained to defend a cause—the cause of the Emperor; to carry out a command—the command of the Emperor, the symbol of their nation.

So, Japan was different and the only force that could meet them head on was the Communist with its equally fervent conviction and single-mindedness in Asia. So it was that Mao became the symbol of a new hope of nationalism for China and Asia.

But the strength of Japan was also the reason for her ultimate failure. Japan, as I have said, did not change her social structure or her civilisation since her armies had been so successful. So she thought in feudal and empirical terms when she struck the West in the Pacific.

Even as she struck through Thailand, another Buddhist land of peace, Malaya, the Philippines and Indonesia with its separate islands, she came with the idea of establishing an empire, an idea which was already out of place in the 20th century. She came with a programme to establish a Greater Co-prosperity Sphere for Asia but with herself as the dominant nation and the rest as subdominant colonial entities.

The idea was out of date, her feudal structure did not allow her to realise this, and thus, despite development in science and technology and her greater discipline, devotion to duty, she lost the war despite or because of her brutality against all.

When Japan invaded the countries of Southeast Asia, she did more than just begin a war against the West. She opened the eyes of the West to the power of the East. More than that, she also opened the eyes of these countries. Though she left the countries divided, she left them with an awareness of their own need to be independent. It would be interesting to speculate what would have been the outcome had she given those countries the freedom they were promised and become their friends. As it turned out, her defeat was only the defeat of another occupying power, more brutal than the one she replaced briefly.

Penang was a remote island of divided peoples when Japan came and opened its eyes to its own abilities and potential and the fact that there could be equal nations between the East and West. Like the rest of the archipelago, Penang was a land of divided peoples. Alas, they were still divided peoples when Japan left.

The fact that the events took place in Penang is not important for it is but a microcosm from which the macrocosm can be discerned.

It is also a typical story of how the people of Southeast Asia responded to the war and directed their energies towards the growth of struggles for independence that were to engulf the entire region from Vietnam down to Indonesia after the war. The war, if it did not bring about unity of the peoples and left them as divided as ever, had sown awareness amongst them of similarities and if we are still divided today, we also know what nationalism is about. For the war sowed the seeds of independence and jelled the nascent feelings of nationalism that had begun to sprout even before the outbreak of war.

I saw one of them that Singapore night,
A symbol of death in silver shape, tinsel bright
Pinned by searchlights against the black sky,
Like a white tree angel on a Christmas night.

It came like an angelic being of beauty
But in stealth and with guilty death.

Now, they glide brazenly into the dawn,
Silver grey wings glowing with red suns,
Turning white the pure blue sky.
Like gulls returning from the sea

But they have come, not for shelter
From cruel winds wracking the seas.
They have come to bring the thunder of fire
The rain of shrapnel, to bring
To an innocent childlike island
Corruption, perversion and death.

1. DEATH OF THE INNOCENTS

EVEN as Japan was massing her forces on the beaches of Southern Thailand with the intention of overrunning the entire Malayan peninsula, and despite the bombing of Singapore on the night of December 7, I was naive enough to believe the propaganda that the Japanese army was too primitive and inferior to take on the British forces. I still had the Mikado caricatures of the Japanese that the English and Italian operas had imaged in my mind.

Come to think of it, I believe I was not the only one who was lulled. In the light of the after events, it would appear that the British High Command might also have been duped by their own propaganda. Either that or ...

For HMS *The Prince of Wales* and the HMS *Repulse* were ordered out of Singapore to meet the Japanese threat without proper air cover but with confidence that they would be able to stem the advance of the invading army who had dared to attempt to take on the forces of the largest Empire the world had ever seen and on which the sun never set, only to be sent to their watery graves some one hundred miles or so from the Japanese landings even as I was on my way from Singapore to Penang in the last train to the north of the peninsula, trusting that the Japanese troops would never breach the Jitra Line.

I arrived home on December 10 to find my father in camp and my mother at home with no one to take charge of the family and to decide if we should prepare for the worst and evacuate to the hills.

Up to that moment, the island had not met the ravages of the war and there had been no air raid though a few planes had flew briefly over the mainland. But there was no doubt that war had come even if we had no idea which direction it would take.

The entire city was filled with wonderment. The lack of preparation had brought about a bewilderment and because no one knew what to do everyone kept asking everyone else what should be done as they wandered from group to concerned group.

The government had not been honest with us. Whilst our defences were in dire straits, assurance after assurance kept coming one after another that everything was in order and that reinforcements were coming. Whether that was good propaganda or not, our defences were crumbling and the Jitra Line to the north of Penang was proving to be no firmer than a sandcastle facing the tide.

We were completely helpless in the face of the advancing Japanese troops that had landed in Thailand who had met no counter action from our forces on the beaches before they consolidated themselves and there seemed to be no deployment to meet the forces which had cut through the isthmus to attack the passive defence line at Jitra.

I did not know what to do after I arrived home. No positive order or suggestions were given to the populace. We did not know if we had to prepare for air raids or to evacuate the city. The policy of having a quiet and non-political people was proving unsound in the light of the new situation. Even if we wanted to, we could do little against a trained army advancing from firm beachheads. The land behind our front at Jitra was completely unprepared even to protect ourselves from an enemy.

At a loss as to what to do, I decided to build an air raid shelter in the morning room of our house, using a corner and its two walls and completing the other two sides with interlocking wooden supports and surrounding the entire shelter with sand bags.

I had no design experience and could only imitate what I had seen from war pictures of London. I was well aware that the shelter I had built would only be good against shrapnel but not a strong blast which could easily push the sandbags in. But that was the best I could do.

I realise now that evacuation would have been best, for in the countryside we stood a better chance against bombing and it was nearer to our food sources, whatever there was, for Penang depended a great deal upon imports. But there had been no plans made by the government at all for such measures.

They had not even asked the people to stock up for emergencies; they did not even give instructions for the food in their godowns and warehouses to be distributed to the people. They just abandoned them to the Japanese. Had the people not helped themselves, all of their provisions would have fallen into the hands of the enemy. It was not as if the provisions would have lasted till they returned.

The morning room was chosen because it was a one-storey structure and the likelihood of being crushed by the weight of the building was less.

My reason for the shelter might have been purely a psychological one. For the best reason for it was that there were no military objectives and I did not think the planes would bomb the city. We were on the outskirts of the city so we were relatively free from the dangers of terror bombing of the city.

I was wrong. On the morning of the 11th, we were bombed. I was in my garden when I heard their engines and then I saw them flying into the island from the Penang channel through the dappled morning sky. Not quite realising what they were intending to do, I looked at them as they came in directly from the sea and passed to my right, aiming at the city.

But there was a premonition, for I did not think they looked pretty any longer. Glowering in the morning light, they flew in perfect formation, the perfect symmetry of their grey shapes looking coldly impressive, the bright round suns below their wings seemingly gloating, their engines beating out a merciless and pitiless mechanical throb. Like ministers of death, heralded by their own engines; like a flock of gulls gliding over food pushed in from the sea by an ocean storm, they came slowly over the coastline towards the centre of Chinatown to spread destruction and panic to a childlike island which had no business in the war and which had known no thunder other than the thunder of the monsoons.

They might have had an excuse to bomb Singapore for it was claimed to be an island fortress of the British Empire. But they had no business to do the same to Penang. It was completely defenceless except for a few pillboxes and a gun emplacement in the South West facing the South at Batu Maung and pointing out to sea in the direction of Singapore which was without any guns. The British had not thought the Japanese would attack through the jungles of the North but would attack the peninsula at Singapore.

The island was full of unwarlike people who had not even been trained for civil resistance. It was full of Babas and Nyonyas who knew no nationality and were happy to be British subjects and whose concern was only with the affairs of themselves and their families and peace on the island that they might prosper.

They had little interest in governing themselves, much less the affairs of war. It was something which was their strength and their weakness.

It was a study in contrasts. The planes were manned by men of determined purpose, hardened through years of war in China and trained for merciless warfare, proud to die for their country. The people of Penang had been taught to be submissive and peace loving and to value their lives.

Twenty-seven planes in all, in three flights of nine planes each, came that morning to bomb Penang, flown by those who knew what they were doing. They would be bombing uncynical people who would stand in wonderment and bewilderment even as the bombs fell around them. They had not been even politically trained and fervently believed that war would not come. If it did the British would blow away the Japanese army like a huge fan would blow away the flies.

The Japanese pilots knew they were on a mission to conquer the entire Far East. They had a mission to present Singapore as a birthday gift to their Emperor on February 15, 1942 and Penang was in the path of their advance to Singapore.

But the Penang they bombed did not really stand in their way for it was not on the mainland over which they would have to go. It was an island which they could easily side step. But that did not seem a consideration. They were determined to bomb it even if it had little military significance in their advance towards Singapore that was their real objective.

Even as the Japanese bombardiers were directing the pilots on to their targets, the people stopped their marketing and gathered to marvel at what was coming towards them. Many even thought they were no more than friendly British planes despatched to protect them from the enemy. So, as the formation of planes closed in to carpet bomb the market area of the Prangin Road, which was the main market of the island, slicing through the air towards their target like a shoal of barracuda going for the kill, Chinatown was packed with innocent victims gathered together in peaceful wonderment.

I am sure the pilots had probably never even heard of the island before, just as those they were about to bomb ever seen a bomber. But, in order to cause the greatest injury and panic, they had selected the most populous area and I have often wondered why carpet bombing has never been classified as a war crime.

From my garden, some two miles from the target area, I heard the ominous rat-tat-tat-tat coming from the planes and wondered if it was the sound of cannon firing or of bombs being released from their racks. I have never been a pilot and so I do not know. But they sounded like cannon shots.

Immediately afterwards, I began to hear the whistling sound of falling bombs. It brought me back to reality for I had read somewhere that falling bombs make whistling sounds. I immediately thought of dropping to the ground only to hesitate when I remembered having been told that when one hears the whistle of a bomb, it is already too late to do anything for the bomb will have passed overhead. It is the bomb one does not hear that is meant for us.

For the thousands at the market, standing and looking up that morning, the bombs did not whistle. They watched with fascination, not knowing what was coming as a shoal of fish would stay still to watch in silence as a fisherman surrounds them with a net, when the bombs began to explode.

Bodies and limbs were blown about everywhere, smashing into walls and beams; bits of masonry and timber flew sky high to dot the sky and blood was splattered everywhere. If the planes had intended to strike terror and cause panic, they certainly succeeded. They had struck at the heart of the city at its most active time. They could not have done more.

A piece of shrapnel symbolically sliced off a few heads from the carving on the green granite centrepiece of the front garden wall of my grandfather's mansion. I have that piece remounted in my garden today with the damage still showing.

By what reason could such wanton destruction have been warranted it is hard to imagine. It did not gain the Japanese an iota of military advantage. Nor did it serve the purpose of proving their military prowess to the people who did not understand war. Her victories would have been sufficient proof of her prowess.

If the intention was to win the hearts and minds of fellow Asians against a Western foe, this was completely unnecessary. We were fellow Asians and colonial subjects. We could easily relate, identify with her. I could not understand it.

Carpet bombing was a scare tactic and panic a legitimate objective; that was what was meant by a total war. But in what way was it not a war crime? Least of all, how could it apply to a people who had no part in the war and who lived on an island with nowhere to run to.

Was Japan just trying to show off her ability as poor men love to show off their new found wealth? The destruction was wanton. It wiped out the innocence of the people forever to no purpose for Japan except that now, the utter ruthlessness and the insensitivity of Japan had been confirmed.

"We who are about to die, salute you!" But the people were not gladiators and they did not know they had to die.

Unable to find any sane reason why Japan had chosen to inflict such injury on innocent people which had little or nothing to do with the war, a local and cynical quip arose.

There were several rows of handcarts parked along the side of the Prangin Road canal in front of the mansion with their handles pointing skyward. They could look like rows upon rows of hostile anti-aircraft guns pointing up at them, the story went. That was why the Japanese had to bomb the area.

Of course, handcarts were handcarts and no intelligent commander of a squadron could have ever mistaken them for anti-aircraft guns even if their handles pointed skyward, even if they were shortsighted. When this was suggested, the answer was another question. Then, why did the Japanese bomb us?

*They were destined to be humble
The proud Imperial nations of the West
Help usher in a new era of emancipation,
Yet they had not thought even to spare
The most innocuous of islands
Nor the innocent children there*

*Who had known no more than the sounds
Of the monsoon winds, its storms and surf.*

*I thought they looked so pretty—
Till the bombs came screaming down
To turn red the golden sands.*

2. I THOUGHT THEY LOOKED SO PRETTY

THE sounds of the exploding bombs that morning did not quite reach our house. So, even as the squadrons peeled off from their run to begin their homeward journey, I did not quite know what had happened.

It was only when the first of the refugees running past my home caught my attention that I began to take notice. They were youths and it was their running that brought about the first misgivings in me. Even then I did not realise the true reason as to why they were running away. I only thought that there had been some sort of a riot or a gang fight that they were running away from.

I was still standing in the garden watching a small column of smoke rise in the direction of Prangin Road and wondering what it was when the hurried patter of footsteps of the first of the panic stricken running past the house drew my attention to the road. I went closer to the fence to have a clearer look.

It was then I realised that the people were running away from the city. They were the first refugees. Many wore slippers and some were barefooted. There were not many at first, only a trickle in their ones and twos and this quickly swelled into a constant trickle even as I watched.

Consumed with curiosity and still assuming that it was not more serious than a riot, I shouted out to one of the youths.

"Why are you running?"

The youth turned to look at me. His face was ashen pale and his eyes filled with disbelief. He kept on running as he looked at me. I could see he was my age and he was terrified beyond reasoning. All he could think of was to run.

His left hand was extended over his left shoulder, pointing towards the smoke rising from the town, speechless with fright and struggling to find his voice. All he could do was to stare at me with unblinking eyes and then someone further down the line called out to answer for him:

"The planes have bombed the town!"

It was only then that I realised what had truly happened. This was a stampede. I looked at the smoke again and it was now obvious that a few fires must have started.

Soon the trickle became a thin stream of panting men, women and children who began to fill the road with cycles, trishaws and handcarts packed with belongings as they ran as fast as they could to put as much distance between themselves and the destruction they had witnessed for fear of the planes returning.

They came brazenly with claims,
Propaganda leaflets floating down,
With claims to set the people free,
Bold red sun emblazoning their silver wings.
Symbols, they claim of boldness and purity,
Their wings in noble silver white.
But their leaflets floated down
With bombs to make red the golden sands.

3. MYTHS AND HYPOCRISIES

THE planes did not return, they had unloaded all their bombs in those few seconds and they were on their way home. But almost the entire city was on the move, concerned only with their own safety. The significance in history that the Japanese military were so proud of that for the first time since Genghis Khan had struck so firmly at the West was lost to them.

I would see a change in world outlook and the fall of Empires, the challenge of an Eastern nation on the West, a witness to the beginning of a tremendous change in history, but all I could see was fear, pain, panic and a stampede.

I went into the house and reported to my mother what I had seen. She was strangely calm and deliberate. But she told me to take the car into the city to see what had happened to her friends.

I went first to Siam Road to see if Swee Eng and Choo Kin, two of my fellow students who had returned with me by the same train and their families who were also friends of my mother were safe and secure. They were. Nevertheless, their front door was bolted and what I saw were anxious faces peering out from behind the lattice work. They did not open the door.

Like everyone else, they were in a state of fear and confusion and did not know what they should do. The bombs had fallen nowhere close but, like everyone else, it was something they had not experienced before and there was no guidance from the government. They did not know what to do.

I had a brief word with them and suggested that they should evacuate the city as it was no longer safe. I suggested that they should think of going up the hill to our house as they had nowhere to run to and there were no males in the house.

But why should they evacuate at all? The mother asked. They had no part in the war. It was a fight between the British and the Japanese and it was no concern of theirs? A strange but rather pertinent question. How should I reply? I told her we were no one's concern, that was the problem. We only happened to stand in the way.

With that I continued my journey into the city to see for myself the mood that had overtaken it. But I did not have to go far. No sooner had I hit one of the main roads, the terror and consternation were obvious. The stampede was already making vehicular traffic difficult.

The streets were full of bicycles, trishaws and even hand carts either haphazardly piled with personal belongings salvaged from homes or filled with the injured and those who were too ill to walk, followed by a stream of distraught refugees, a compelling scene of the reality of war.

To the steady rumble and the steady roll of cart wheels came the sounds of weeping and moaning as relatives accompanied the injured, the dead and the dying to the General Hospital where hope for help could be obtained.

Sometimes the weeping and moaning were punctuated by the occasional shouting and the thud of despairing women desperately beating at the sides of carts as it was discovered that the cart was carrying someone who had just expired.

I was at the Serengeti plains in 1978 at the season of the drought and mass migration of the animals as they sought to reach the more sustaining fertile wet lands to the South. There I saw the hunter and the hunted, wildebeest, antelope, deer, zebra, elephants and giraffes moving together with the lion and the hyena oblivious of one another, concentrated only in fleeing the life threatening drought.

There was only the silent thunder of hoofs and clouds of dust as the animals pressed against one another in their anxiety to move away as fast as they could. It reminded me of what I saw in the city that morning.

The exodus was uncontrolled but for the direction they were going, onwards and onwards towards the life succouring hills. No action had been taken to pacify the crowds and the roads and junctions were unmanned by the police. The people moved only by primitive instinct to find safety.

Leadership was wanted, if only to control the flow of the exodus which filled all the three main roads out of the city. It seemed as if the police had been rendered incapable. Perhaps, they too were busy evacuating their own families.

The panic-stricken crowds, some of whom were already trying to stop my car for a lift, soon compelled me to the conclusion that it was futile to continue my journey.

The government appeared to be in much the same state of shock as the rest of the city. In an emergency this was least to be expected of a responsible government. It was unworthy of Britain, an indignity she could never live down. I went to the General Hospital on my way home. The sight that greeted me was something out of a horror film. Though it was only soon after the bombing, the hospital and its corridors and approaches were already full to the brim with the dead and wounded to whom help could possibly never come in time.

The bombs had torn many a limb from its body and many had missing parts. The dying and the dead were intermingled in the corridors because there were so many of them. Even as I looked, more of the injured were being brought in. But the place was full and the handcarts and trishaws could not off load their passengers because there was no place to off load them to. So everyone had to wait their turn, if it should ever come.

In the meantime, all the help they got was the succour and hope given them by crying relatives who could do no more than add to the misery by weeping and crying as they waited helplessly and patiently for help in vain.

Inside the hospital, the chaos was just as bad, but at least things were moving. Nurses were helping to dress wounds and administer pain killers and the operating theatre was overflowing. Both it and the casualty ward were crowded with patients waiting for their turn on the operating table.

But it was heartening to see that the hospital was still functioning. The reason became obvious later. The Medical Superintendent of the General Hospital, I believe, was a Dr Evans. He was the only one who did not desert his post. He refused to be evacuated and stayed back on duty till his post was taken over by a Japanese Medical Officer a few weeks later. It was he who maintained order and control over the Hospital throughout. He worked hard and unremittingly that first day and thereafter, to mend and give succour to the bomb injured patients in the hospital. I am not sure of his name but the record books should put this straight. He should not have been forgotten and ought to have been honoured and it is unfortunate that he has not been so honoured. If anyone should be recognised for maintaining the best of British traditions in the face of utmost danger, it surely could only have been this unrecognised Medical Superintendent.

Though the Hospital was overworked and unable to cope with the torrent of injured, order and this sense of direction were not reflected elsewhere. Thanks have to be offered to the hospital, its nurses and the voluntary workers who continued their duties in the face of danger and deprivation. But the rest of the government was in apparent chaos and it seemed that the government officers themselves were in an equal state of shock.

They would have had better access to the news from the war front and must have known of the speed of the Japanese advance. It was obvious that the planes would return and that the island was defenceless and something should be done about getting the people out of the city.

But the prospect must have been frightening enough to render the entire government machinery moribund for no guidance ever came nor was any public announcement made as to what the populace should do or not do.

They were no longer leaders and therefore no longer capable of ruling. It seemed that they were also waiting for instructions to evacuate which they were to do surreptitiously two days later. Of course, we did not know this till after they had gone.

Was Perry to blame for forcing open
The doors of Japan and letting loose
The samurai hounds of wrath who would
One day seek to humble the West
With vengeful sword and change the face
Of Asia and awaken a sleeping dragon?

4. THE EVACUATION

NAKED fear was everywhere. Each one was looking after himself and the glue of society, never strong, had turned to no more than sticky streaks. No one, except the brave little band of nurses and their volunteers who were working alongside them at the hospital, had time to think of the others.

I had to think of evacuating the family from the city. I turned the car homewards and we began to pack our things. Ah Boon, the cook, refused to leave with us. He was taken in as a young boy when he came from China and had been a long time with us. He had run away from China during the turmoil of the civil war and knew what it was to lose a home. He was going nowhere. He would stay back in the house even if he could not do anything but hide should the Japanese come into the house.

I chose the hill because it was the only place I could think of and because everyone was in agreement. My father being away in camp, I thought Claremont would be safe.

That was how I happened to have had a ringside view of the brief dogfight between the Buffaloes and the bombers which returned the next day to release propaganda pamphlets as well.

Again, I happened to be outside in the garden when the planes returned. This time, from the vantage point of the hill I could see how low the planes were flying for, though I was but about 1,400 feet up, the planes seemed to be flying almost at eye level. This was on December 13.

The two single seater fighter Buffaloes stationed across at Butterworth gallantly rose to meet them when they came into sight. It was a gallant but a pitiable sight. The planes took off too late. It was as if the entire pantomime was put up to confirm the might of Japan.

The bomber bringing up the rear of the bomber formation, peeled off as soon as the two Buffaloes raced their engines to take to the air one after the other, climbing to reach a height for a suitable attack. The bomber went into a shallow dive and caught the first Buffalo almost laconically even as it banked in a move to go behind the bomber and with the first burst of its guns sent the fighter into a spiral before it plunged into the ground in a plume of smoke.

Even as the first plane began to plunge, the bomber was already turning towards the second fighter, also trying to gain height. As it approached the Buffalo, the Buffalo turned tail and fled off in a southerly direction and I was told later that it reached Ipoh before it landed safely. I believe the pilot lived to tell a sad tale.

One could begin to see the absurdity of wars. In a way, it is a pantomime, if only there were no tragedy of innocents. But it is the innocents who suffered.

As for me, I consider myself one of the innocents. A victim of war as well as a victim of colonialism. I believed in British might and superiority. Even after the bombs fell in Singapore, I still believed in the superior might of the British armed forces as did many of us who became volunteers and fought with the British forces to the end.

In my case, my trust and innocence let me board the last train from Singapore to Penang on the night of December 9. It was the same trust and innocence that my college friends from up country boarded the same train, with their parents' blessings, not realising that we would only be riding the journey up into what was seen to be enemy occupied territory. We were to suffer for this innocence.

As with the mystery of why nations go to war, so also the mystery why there was the belief of the earlier centuries that it was profitable to build and hold on to colonies. Was it really profitable or was it due to the need to prove one's sense of superiority or self-righteousness? For in both cases one has to cope with hostility and to cultivate the myth of superiority, an irksome habit which is tiresome to maintain.

In this case, the result of this inculcation had led to a sense of inferiority in the people and a habitual pretence of greatness amongst the British personnel which would make it difficult for them to stomach the humiliation of defeat brought about by the Japanese whose prowess became exaggerated in the minds of the people who had come to accept the greatness of the British Empire on which the sun would never set.

The vanities of colonialism had come home to roost. When Japan bombed the island, they did more than rip open buildings, plaster walls with bits of human flesh and turn the streets red with blood. They shook the innocence out of our eyes. They also shook the myth of British superiority and invincibility of the Empire to their roots, destroying the myth of Western racial superiority.

The emotional victory was all the more intense, and the fear shown by the entire British government of Penang emphasised, when the people saw with their own eyes the ease with which a bomber shot down a British fighter and put the other to flight.

The feet of clay were exposed and their surreptitious departure could only elevate the admiration of the Japanese in the eyes of the people.

The evacuation of the entire government of Penang and the way it was done have always been a mystery. No doubt, there was good reason for the evacuation as Penang was defenceless. But surely not in the way it was done with no one left behind even to formally surrender the city to the Japanese. There was no reason why they had to flee in the mist of midnight in silence.

There has been no inquiry and no clear evidence as to who gave the command for the entire government of Penang to be evacuated and in such a manner. But evacuation must have been in the minds of the officers from the very first day. This would probably account for the way the public duties of the Penang government were executed even from the very first bombing. But until they had evacuated few knew that it was taking place.

Lim Khoon Teik, a Singaporean, was then the only senior non-European in the service. He was a King's Scholar and an officer in the colonial legal service who had been seconded to serve as the senior First Class magistrate in the state. It was a position of high honour and, as a Singaporean, was entitled to be evacuated with the rest of the European community.

As a matter of fact, he had also been served with a secret order to present himself no later than twelve midnight that day at Swettenham Pier with only immediate members of his family, which meant his Chinese Singaporean wife for they were without children and their essential personal belongings.

Though evacuation was not specifically mentioned the import of the missive was clear. Just before midnight, he presented himself there with his wife. There he found almost the entire European population of the island and waiting for them was the entire fleet of cross channel ferries.

At the stroke of midnight, all those assembled began to board the ferries. But, to his surprise, he was not allowed to board. He protested vehemently but was told that the order had been sent to him in error. It was a circular meant only for whites and the boats were full.

He remonstrated. His rank as an officer of the volunteers as well as a civilian officer from Singapore entitled him to evacuation. But he was pushed aside and told in no uncertain terms that he was not white and therefore not allowed to board and that the order sent to him to evacuate had been sent in error.

Thus he was the most senior man left on the island. But no last minute instructions were given to him as to how he should deal with the island and if he was to surrender it to the Japanese.

Stunned, he watched the entire contingent cast off and sail into the midnight mists in silence and in stealth.

Another man had been left behind. It was Dr Evans who refused to leave his post and maintained British dignity to the last. He was carted off to a prisoner-of-war camp. The rest of his history is not known to me.

That was how the British government left Penang. They had lost for Britain the pride and the dignity of the Empire. How could they ever, after that, think to indict anyone for treason?

The Empire had bowed and fled in ignominy.

The next morning the entire island woke as if into a bad dream. But the time for tears was over. The myth was gone, the reality was that the people had to look for their own leadership. The people grew up at once. In a way, one can cynically say that of a new birth. With it came a new people with a different perception of the world and themselves. A new awareness was thus thrust upon them and a new people with faith in themselves was born.

The colour of the Pacific sky was blue,
The colour of its peaceful sun white,
The colour of the innocent sand was gold,
But the silver wings of their planes
Dirtied the blue sky, their red suns
Blotted out the white sun and their bombs
Turned the azure seas incarnadine

5. RAISE THE WHITE FLAG

WHEN the planes returned the next day, it was to a deserted forgotten island. Though there was no need for it, propaganda pamphlets were dropped, ridiculing an enemy that was no longer there.

As the formation turned back, a lone bomber left the formation to come low over Penang Hill to drop a bomb near the top station. Whether it was meant for Bel Retiro, the official hill station residence of the British Resident Commissioner nearby or for the engine room of the top section, we do not know. But a shrapnel of the bomb which fell on the jungle nearby, hit the engine house to put the railway temporarily out of commission.

It was Saravanamuthu (the then editor of the *Straits Echo* which belonged to my uncle) who thought it was time someone told the Japanese army the truth so that the bombing and further useless slaughter be stopped after the planes had left that morning. He was one of the two who had the initiative to do something in the vacuum left by the British to stop the further bombing of the island, even if it was to raise the white flag of surrender. Taking courage in both his hands, he asked someone to climb the fort to the flag pole to raise a white flag of surrender. The fort was Fort Cornwallis the site of the landing of Francis Light, hence dimming the lights over a symbol of British supremacy.

It is not difficult to see that raising a white flag of surrender could be read as an act of surrender which required the consent of His Majesty (at that time the ruling monarch was King George VI) and that he had done that on his personal decision was an act of great courage. He was to become the permanent representative for an independent Ceylon (as Sri Lanka was known at that time) after the war.

At the same time, a young Eurasian horse trainer, with equal initiative but with stronger determination, chose to cycle all the twenty-one miles to Sungei Petani, where the Japanese front line headquarters was, to inform the enemy that the British government had evacuated the island and that it was now defenceless.

They both deserved equal credit for what they did. They might have saved many lives for the planes never returned to bomb the city again nor were reprisals taken on the populace by the Japanese occupation troops as they did in Singapore. Their acts were creditable and heroic but neither was recognised for their acts of courage nor was their initiative taken into account after the war.

There were others too who acted bravely and with self-sacrifice at that time, such as my father and Lim Khoon Teik after recovering from his disappointment of being left behind during the evacuation. They too, were men of the moment, displaying in their acts altruism and concern for others and of their own society when their services were needed. Of them I shall have more to say later.

On the morning of the discovery of the British evacuation, those who were still undecided if they should leave the city made up their minds that they should leave the city to the Japanese troops whom they expected to come in as soon as the evacuation was made known to them.

Georgetown is on a promontory of the island. Many of its inhabitants did not have country homes or relatives in the hinterland. Many had nowhere to go. But, nevertheless, those who could leave, left for the suburbs and the foothills of the central island chain.

Thus, the suburbs swelled, pushing the late comers further inland towards Thean Teik and the Khoo Kongsi estates towards the Ayer Itam village and beyond towards Paya Terubong on the foothills of Penang Hill. There were those who even had to go as far as the back of the island to Balik Pulau and its environs—the girls shedding their hair and donning their brothers' clothes and even going to the extent of becoming peasant farmers in the hope of escaping the Japanese soldiers whose rapacious character had long preceded them.

As the suburbs swelled, expanding the city limits quickly, the city was emptied of its human contents. The hitherto quiet countryside began to resound with the hustle and bustle of humanity and shrill human voices began to pierce the quiet of the hills, turning the small village of Ayer Itam and its market, which traditionally acted only as the market for products of the surrounding hills, almost into a metropolis.

Penang Hill, too, which the train serviced and where Bel Retiro was situated, was not spared the refugees. Unfortunately, the bombing of the top station reduced drastically the flow of refugees as it was not easy for city folk to walk up the hill. As long as there was a functioning railway the lucky were able to proceed their stately way up the hill by train. But after the bombing, the traffic ceased, saving the bungalows up the hill from overcrowding.

When the train was put back into service a few weeks later, the evacuation had ceased and the people moved back into the plain.

I happened to be at the middle station soon after the bomb fell. I believe it was because I was there that my life during the war took a distinctive direction. For, until that time, I was not sure what I was going to do.

That morning, I chanced to come across a daughter-in-law of Yeap Chor Ee, the Rockefeller of Penang and the owner of Ban Hin Lee Bank. Eda Oei was someone whose beauty I had always admired. A Chinese Indonesian, she was one of the daughters of Oei Teong Ham, the sugar king of Indonesia and the benefactor of Yeap Chor Ee himself.

They had become friends and he decided to marry two of his daughters to two of the sons of Yeap Chor Ee and she was one of them. She was one of the late evacuees who had decided to come up the hill too late. She was on her way up when the engine room was hit and she found herself stranded at the middle station with her *amah* and her little son in her arms.

The Bank had a house up the hill where the rest of the family, including Yeap Chor Ee himself, had gone to earlier and she was on her way to join them when the engine room of the upper section of the railway was hit. She was quite distraught and at a loss as to what she should do, loaded as she was with her baby, his *amah*, his milk and its bottle, diapers and all.

Knowing who she was, I explained that there was no hope that the train would ever be repaired on time. No one could be found for its repair in the situation. She had no alternative but to walk the rest of the way up.

I should have suggested that she ask one of the workers there if he could help her up but I did not think of it, probably because the British were very strict about any of its servants being otherwise employed. Instead, my gallantry taking the better part of my valour, I offered my help.

Before I could change my mind, this offer was immediately accepted with relief. So I found myself carrying the baby who was already at the age when he was big enough to start learning how to walk but had not done so. He was heavier than I thought and I was to regret my gallantry only too soon.

We had hardly reached our Claremont station when I found lifting myself up the steps of the railway threatening to be impossible as he seemed to grow heavier and heavier as if he was taking delight in my predicament. By the time I had reached our station he had become a heavyweight.

But I could not give up, my pride was in my way. Fortunately, she was not used to hill climbing herself either and we took a breather at the station itself. After that, there was nothing else but a slow progress up the tracks to the top station with one laborious step after another, punctuated by frequent rests. After what seemed like hours, we finally reached our destination, my pride and gallantry still intact even if I was huffing and puffing.

At the house the drink offered was welcomed. The house was full of people and Yeap Chor Ee himself was sitting in an easy chair in the front hall. He did not come out nor did I go in but stood by the doorway to catch my breath and to observe the style and nature of the family.

It was there that I suddenly discovered what I could do for the duration of the war. Like every household I was to meet on the hill, the war had caught the family without provisions in the larder and I could at once see myself in the role of a food supplier.

No one had expected war and the rapid advance of the Japanese army and so no one had made provision for it. The bungalows up the hill were weekend bungalows and food was normally brought up by the weekenders. The larders were never full and it was obvious that food would soon become a problem.

This was obvious but from the questions put to me when I arrived at her house it seemed that nothing was further from their mind. Strangely, they would not believe what was obvious. The British army had been defeated and it would be a long while before the Japanese would be driven from the island. Till then, tinned provisions, which were essential for such households, would no longer come from Britain and they should, if they were wise, think of getting hold of some whilst the stocks lasted or find alternatives.

Yeap Chor Ee sitting in the living room a short distance away and within earshot, without stirring from his chair and acting as if he was not listening, took it all in.

I explained that they should at once look for places in the jungle to hide should Japanese soldiers come up the hill, for they would not stay long up the hill, there being no reason to. And in the meanwhile, they should begin to stock up their larder for there was nowhere one could buy anything up the hill but some farm produce.

I could see there was a lack of leadership and they were looking to me for suggestions as to what they should do. In a way, it was pathetic to see so many grown-ups so lost. That is, if one discounted the grand old man Yeap Chor Ee himself. For he was a great leader and very used to the power of money. He would no doubt buy himself out of any predicament he would find himself in.

But one thing was certain, no one in that household was about to risk his life and limb and this helped me make up my mind. I would become their supplier. I would go down the hill the next day and bring what I could with my bare hands and sell what I could. In that way, my ten dollars, which was all I had in the world, would slowly grow.

"The best you all could do is look for a safe place for the women to hide themselves in should Japanese troops come up the hill," I suggested, by way of ending the conversation. There was immediate silence. Perhaps they had other plans.

"There are plenty of caves and streams where there are hiding places," I continued. "Should there be an emergency, spread out so that not all of you would be found out at the same time."

I suddenly realised why there was silence. My emergency plans spelled danger and that was not palatable and they did not want to hear it. But there was nothing else. Confronted with the unfamiliar their imagination could not comprehend it and they were hoping that they would not have to come to that situation. They were also still, in a state of shock. Perhaps they would understand it later but not yet.

"It is also important that you begin to stock up some food at once whilst stocks are still available," I added, thinking of myself. "Soon there will be no more. There's no knowing how long we are going to stay up here. How's your stock position?" That question was met with a blank stare. I knew their cupboard was bare and was only stressing their desperate situation to make it easier to introduce myself later as their supplier of food.

But I could also see that I could kill two birds with one stone, feed them and look after myself at the same time. I was young and still thought in simple terms. Supply them with what they needed. That way I could help them. But at the same time I could help myself too.

My ten dollars was all that was left after my return from Singapore. My father was then still away and all the British banks of which he was a customer had shut down for the duration and there was little chance that he could find any money.

But my intention was not entirely altruistic. Faced with uncertainty and starvation, it was the best I could think of. Much as I wanted to help, I could also help myself. It would be fair exchange and could mean my family's survival as well, should the war go on.

I had neither experience nor qualification except that I had been taught to be independent by my parents and, in that way, I suppose, meeting them decided for me my role in the war.

I left them, promising to return with what I could find at the foot of the hill at Ayer Itam. On my way down the hill to our house, I did a quick detour to take a look around to see what the situation was like and the size of my "market".

The general feeling on the hill was the same. Everyone was interested to stock up but none was willing to go down the hill without the train. Someone would have to do the needful and I could not see why that someone could not be me.

My visit to the Ban Hin Lee household was also helpful in another way. For the first time I was able to look at myself in relation to others who were in need. I could see a different outlook. I could see myself not only in isolation but as part of a society on whose health ours depended.

It was our upbringing that had been different. It had made me, or my family, outward looking, with a sense of responsibility towards the general good and we were not afraid to do what was right.

Now, under conditions of war, this difference was making an immediate impact. We were not afraid of venturing forth whilst others hesitated.

This spirit would be better illustrated by what my father and Lim Khoon Teik and his slim band of volunteers were about to do in the village of Ayer Itam and the yeoman service they would put in.

That was also how my ten dollars were to launch me on my wartime journey. Not withstanding my lack of experience and the paucity of my capital, I would, I resolved, go down to the village to see what I could buy to bring up the hill and thus begin this journey.

From a student, I had suddenly become a young man with plans for the future. But I was still moving by instinct, reacting without understanding the meaning of war. My political thinking was still immature and nascent, not capable of encompassing the deeper issues and meaning of war.

I had still to mature, to understand it and to think ideologically. But the time was not yet. Nor would it begin to mature till I had experienced the actuality of war and its conflicts.

In a war, the weak is shown no mercy
Nor are the innocent, nor the proud spared.
The truth is that there are none, such
As the noble or the knave, but only those
Who fight and survive to become the heroes
Or those who refuse or who fumble
Those who may not want to fight and survive
Who are called the cowards or knaves.

One must either kill or be killed
And be honoured and forgotten,
For such is the nature of war.

6. THE NATURE OF WAR

MEANWHILE, even as we were returning to Penang from Singapore, the two British battleships, the aircraft carrier *Repulse* and the battle cruiser *HMS The Prince of Wales*, claimed to be "invincible" and "unsinkable", which had steamed into Singapore a few days before the outbreak of War, were sent out to sea to search and destroy the invading Japanese forces.

The blame apparently was put on Winston Churchill who was rumoured to have sent out the ships without fighter escort against the advice of the Admiralty. Again, this was no more than another attempt to put the blame on someone else for Churchill could not have acted without advice. In any event, the battleships were in Singapore and there was no other alternative but to send them into battle. After all, that was what they were supposed to do. The only question is if the battle plan was the correct one.

Despite the fact that the impending war must have been obvious to those who should have known, our airfields were inadequately prepared and, though there were no large scale attacks on our aerodromes we hardly had any air force to talk of.

There was an Air Chief Marshal, Sir Brooke Popham, the Commander-in-Chief Far East, in Singapore at that time but, to be fair, Britain was at that time fighting for her life and the German army was at the throat of Cairo and all available military power had to be where it was most important to have them, in Europe. What did he have to fight with? There was hardly any aircraft even to attack the Japanese land forces, not to speak of an air cover for the battleships and the presence of only the two Buffalo aircraft at Butterworth airfield at the time of the Japanese bombing of Penang speak for themselves—they were outmoded planes even at that time.

The sinkings were unfortunate because of the effect they brought about. All lingering doubts of Japanese superiority died with the news of those sinkings. Japan had sent the pride of the British Navy to the bottom of the South China Sea. This was a tremendous blow. The unsinkable had been sunk and the invincible had been overcome by the belittled Japanese.

HMS *The Prince of Wales* and HMS *Repulse* had sailed under the command of a Rear Admiral Tom Phillips. Perhaps I would not have remembered this name had I not had the impression that the Japanese were midgets which reduced the sinkings to Lilliputian dimensions, rendering Tom Phillips to the size of a Tom Thumb in my mind.

Instructed to go out on a search-and-destroy mission, he had set sail with no air cover, too late to stop the invasion but not late enough to avoid the Japanese bombers sent to look for him. The planes apparently, according to Japanese sources, were at the limit of their range and were about to turn back when the white wakes of the battleships caught the attention of one of the pilots and immediately, the shortage of fuel notwithstanding, the planes pressed home their attack. The hunters had become the hunted.

This was the first time that we had heard of the term *kamikaze*. Properly translated it means the "divine wind". The *kamikaze* pilots were supposed to aim their planes and themselves with their full load of bombs at their targets. It meant suicide.

That morning, some of the Japanese pilots did just that. Some of the planes were hit as they were diving at their targets and blew up or plunged into the sea; some managed to hit their targets and many of them failed to reach base safely and had to ditch into the sea, short of fuel. But they had achieved their objective and within the hour, the two battleships were crippled and sunk.

According to British sources, the ships were struck and sunk by torpedoes but Japanese sources has it that the ships were first put out of action by the *kamikaze* pilots one of whom dove into the funnel of one of the ships, before they were finally sunk by torpedoes. Whatever the correct version was or if they were both correct was not as relevant as the fact that they had been sunk by Japanese planes. The ships were crippled within the hour and in less than two hours, they had disappeared into the sea with the loss of some 600 lives out of a total crew of 2,900 hands. There was no mercy, such is the nature of war. The weaker is eliminated.

Don't sound the trumpets,
The dead cannot hear
The victors are too drunk
And the maimed and injured
Find the sounds too painful.

The voices you hear are not
Of any applause but cries of pain,
The whimperings and pleas
Of the dying turned to curses.

So, don't blow the trumpets or
Trample on the bleeding roses.

7. THE VOICES YOU HEAR

THE Japanese established beachheads on the beaches of South Thailand even as another army marched into the country from the north, thus threatening the whole of Thailand and forcing the Thai King to capitulate immediately for Buddhist Thailand was not a fighting nation.

Having established beachheads in South Thailand without meeting any resistance, the Japanese assault troops moved swiftly out of Singora across the isthmus of Kra, instead of moving directly south to take the East coast town of Kota Bahru, it took the Jitra Line by circumvention and with a frontal assault. And within a week, the Jitra Line and its huge Indian corps had ceased to exist and was past Penang island on the way to Ipoh and beyond.

According to the Chief of Staff, Matsunobe Tsuji, he had trained the attacking force secretly in Manchuria, mustered it in Taiwan and had boldly sailed across the Gulf of Thailand to land on its East coast.

The West could not have been taken by surprise without anyone being court-marshalled. Either that or we were not ready and had not enough resources and had existed on bluster.

She hit Hawaii also with apparent surprise though we had been warned by a double agent in Japan called "Sorge". She struck Hawaii when the trade wind was firm and on Sunday and when some officers of the American navy were readying themselves for their Sunday golf.

Even her invasion of the Malayan peninsula was calculated with precision. December was the time when the monsoon winds would have been over, the rains would have abated, the seas calm and the sky would be shining. She struck at Bangkok overland from the north even as she prepared to establish beachheads in Singora with the intention to take Singapore, not by sea as expected, but by land from the north.

From the very first moment, she had been successful. Their assault troops which had been trained in Manchuria and secretly mustered in Taiwan for the invasion of Malaya had met no resistance in their landings.

By invading Malaya to take Singapore from the rear, she had apparently wrong footed the British defence which had thought she would attack the island fortress from the sea to the south.

The Jitra Line was our only defence but it was built seemingly with the mentality of those who were responsible for the Maginot Line and it was also breached in the same way, by a lightning and a flanking movement.

The Line had no depth and once cut through and circumvented by little groups going through jungle paths and estate roads on bicycles through the night and even through the rain, the defenders soon found themselves surrounded and unable to mount any counter offensive.

The Jitra Line was manned by the 3rd Indian Corps under Lt General Lewis Heath whose headquarters was not anywhere near the front but halfway down the peninsula in Kuala Lumpur!

The main assault launched three days after landing broke through the lines and by the fourteenth, both the Indian army and the augmenting two British regiments, the East Surreys and the Leicesters had ceased to exist and the way down the peninsula was wide open.

We do not know if there were any British officers at the front for it was the luckless Colonel Gilani, an Indian British Army officer, who had to surrender the bulk of the entire Indian Army which had been manning the Jitra Line.

How well trained the Indian forces were, we would never know, for they hardly fired a shot before they were cut off and had to surrender *en masse*.

According to the book by Matsunobe Tsuji, written after the war, a Japanese force of 25,000 men had taken on and defeated within a little space of time, an army of 75,000 men.

Since there were hardly any Indian servicemen who surrendered in Singapore, we must assume that they were put out of action in Jitra. They were under the command of Colonel Gilani who seemed to have been the most senior officer present since it was he who surrendered his forces.

As for our air force, we have only to refer to Ian Morrison who has this to say in his book on the campaign, "... during the whole Malayan campaign, the Japanese used a total of only 500 planes. ... this figure probably errs on the generous side. ... It was not that the Japanese were strong. It was we ourselves who were weak."

I was in Penang at the time of the invasion. At one moment, I was in the front line, ready for any fighting. The next moment I was behind the front line, in enemy territory. All the news I heard was retreat after retreat and there never was any stand I can talk of proudly.

If there was any air action it was the shambles presented by the two Buffaloes. Like Ian Morrison when he said, "I came away from Singapore in an angry, tempestuous mood, feeling that Malaya and Singapore deserved to go. ... They had drifted complacently along." I, too, felt equally strongly.

The pity was that an entire Indian army had no chance and were forced to surrender without even firing a shot for no good reason at all but poor management.

Japan had reason to be proud of herself. She was to go on down the peninsula, carving her way into Singapore which Yamashita had promised to deliver to his Emperor on his birthday on February 15, 1942 as a birthday gift. Though she had reason to be proud, did she deserve it? The answer is no and this is what this book has to say.

Though we were forced to admire the resolution, determination and the adroit way their troops moved, behind the battle lines, her political thinking did not match her military prowess. She thought in feudal and empirical terms, more pertinent to the wars of old when the conquering of territories and people were for slaves and booty.

This can be seen in her claim that Singapore was to be no more than a birthday present to the Emperor when she claimed to have come to set the people free. Nor can we imagine that the Emperor was interested in that gift as a gift or that he had ever shown any delight in the wars and the annexation of Korea and Manchuria.

Perhaps a land hungry Japan needed space for her hungry people, but surely the idea of using military force for the acquisition of new territory could only have been the result of military thinking. Nor can we say that the conquest of overcrowded China, the rape and plunder and the sacking of cities can in any way be taken as acquisition of land and green pastures. In fact, it is difficult to understand who was responsible even if we know why she went to war unless the individual and his emotional nature is thrown into the argument.

Once this is accepted, we can only conclude that war comes because the person or persons responsible have viewed the situation according to his nature and nature of the culture and civilisation influencing him since no one views a situation that is not coloured by his conditioning and concepts.

And in Japan, it was the nature of the feudal militarists and the culture that gave its ruling class its feudal ego, complex and narrow nationalism. Certainly the Emperor could not have been aware of the crudity and the racist views of the army.

At least in the wars of Greece and Rome where booty women were considered booty of war, Helen of Troy and Cleopatra did provide the inspiration and romance where in the case of the comfort homes, it was absent.

The days of Empires were over, yet they came with the concept of a Greater Co-prosperity Sphere, an ideology that was not only out of date but not understood by her army. They came only to seize whatever they could and there was no talk of winning the hearts of the people and spheres of influence.

Rather than winning the hearts and minds of the people through spheres of ideological influence, their *Kempeitai* used the persuasion of torture and maiming.

If Japan had made Asia proud of the prowess of her armies, her armies also made us ashamed of Japan for their brutality and inhumanity. Steeped in feudalism, Shintoism and Bushido, and encrusted with the inflexibility of military thinking and their belief in the power of the sword which had seen them through so many victories and conquests, they were doomed to failure in the end. For they did not even seem to understand such simple things as humanity and decency, dignity, sensitivity and gentleness.

Most of all, I believe, like most Asians, they did not seem to know the meaning of democracy, the respect for the rights of others and the need to give way or even to surrender power.

Of course, I could be wrong. There were also those Japanese who did not agree with the army. There were those who were as decent as you and I. But I am generalising, knowing fully well that, as in all generalisations, there are always exceptions.

It was all these that forfeited Japan's right to be one of the modern world's most respected states.

*Even in the bold front of war, we often
See the irony, the puny man of history.
The conscript, the mercenary, the eunuch,
The flatterer concerned with himself,
Doing the killing, ignorant of the issues,
Who thinks himself great but is
Nothing but a caricature after all.*

8. PUNY MAN OF HISTORY

BEFORE we actually saw the Japanese soldier in the flesh, he was a political creature of the cartoon, a short, yellow, buck toothed, bowlegged caricature of comic opera, and a figure made inhuman by propaganda which the Rape of Nanking made fearful.

One morning, a few days after stories of rape had given dire warning of their presence on the island, news that Japanese soldiers were coming up the hill quickly spread alarm amongst the refugees and, at Claremont, we began to look for the caves in which to take cover.

I happened to have returned up the hill from Ayer Hitam when the news came. A messenger was despatched to those living further up the hill to look for cover. I went down towards Lower Claremont which was closer to the railway so I could have a better view of the soldiers as they came up the rail track and to prepare the inmates to evacuate as well.

By then the soldiers were already at the middle station. The portion from that station upwards having been put out of action by the bombing of the hill, they had to walk up the tracks and so I positioned myself where I could see if they would go past our Claremont station or turn away from the tracks towards our house in which event we would begin to evacuate the house.

I soon heard rough and guttural voices from my vantage point. They were not the voices of the all conquering heroes of the Hollywood films but peasant voices.

They slowly came into view as they came near the station. Obviously they were not used to climbing hills either, for they seemed to be labouring and cursing as well. It was a group of four or five men, sweaty, bedraggled and in illfitting uniforms. They were the Japanese soldiers themselves.

They had peak cloth caps with flaps hanging over their necks to prevent the sun and the rain from hitting their necks—practical and cheap. A flask was slung round everyone of them which was secured by their belts from which they took a drink once in a way. Apart from their rifles and bayonets, they also had a tin container which carried their ration of rice for the day.

They wore what looked like rubbersoled boots strapped to gaiters into which the bottoms of their trousers were pushed so that they were ready for the mud and the slush of tropical rain.

What struck me most was the contrast between uncouthness and the efficiency of savage power. I had always seen British troops in their resplendent uniforms and boots polished to a shine and had thought that was how a conquering army should look, not such nondescript expendable peasant-like soldiers in expendable-looking clothes.

Of course, they were what efficient fighting troops in the tropics and jungle should look; expendable men in expendable uniforms and provided with what they would require should they survive the day of battle.

But they were what they were supposed to be, no-nonsense fighters. Their entire outfit was for ease of battle, basic and to the point. Even their cloth caps with their flaps and their polo-type trousers were made for easy movement through grass and underbrush. Their clothes were made for easy disposal and burial. They might not have the parade ground polish and might look like cats at play, but they were deadly jungle cats.

At the station, they caused a bit of anxiety as they rested. But, after a while, to my immense relief, instead of turning off to our house, they continued straight up the hill, grumbling and cursing in the hot sun.

The rail tracks just beyond our station went over a shallow valley of a height of some 300 feet or so. When they were somewhere towards the middle of the viaduct, one of them decided to relieve himself and without much ado, turned towards the sun away from the track, unbuttoned his trousers and let fly a stream of golden urine which sparkled in the sun before ending in the trees below.

Then another soldier decided to follow suit. They did not think it funny, nor did they care if anyone was watching them. It was a natural thing but which few cultured people would do. I could not help laughing in comic relief. It was so incongruous.

Here were the all-conquering heroes, about to go up to the Residency up the hill to desecrate a British symbol of supremacy, doing what children who cannot hold their water would do. Who and what were they? Peasants who had been conscripted for a fight and booty or those with a vision and a sense of mission?

Slowly they continued their ascent, watched by nonplussed hidden watchers on the hill attempting their first glance at soldiers who had humbled the British Crown. It was their first sight of the Japanese soldier.

"*Alamak!* They look like us!" That exclamation reverberated around the island. The hill farmers and their families suddenly realised that they too could be the same if not with the same crudity.

The soldiers also looked like peasants. Were such the people who had swept everything before them? Shades of Genghis Khan and his hordes of uncivilised horsemen who rode through the mandarin courts of China and swept through into Persia and beyond, laying down everything that stood in their way even if they had little culture.

Alamak is an extremely useful and expressive local expression, and I have been tempted to use it because it so aptly describes the general feelings then. *Alamak* variously means "My God" as an expression of surprise. Depending on whether it is said in an upward or downward tone, it can also express happy surprise or despondent acceptance of the inevitable. In an undulating tone, it means a querulous "Is that so? Let's see what happens."

In this case, all these meanings apply. The people were genuinely surprised. They were surprised to find that the British were not so superior after all if they could be defeated by such simple-looking people. They were relieved because they did not look like ogres and therefore could be measured by normal standards. Yet, if they looked like us, could they not be brothers? Do brothers fight brothers?

The soldiers soon disappeared from view and this was what happened according to all who saw them, the station workers, the labourers and the hidden people.

They went through the top station and then began to spread out around the playing ground before looking into the deserted police station before they finally went into Bel Retiro (the official Residence up the hill and the symbol of British aloofness and grandeur into which the ordinary local mortals were never invited and to which the Queen was to visit after the war to consecrate the sacrosanct) to desecrate its rooms and toilets with their boots and their dirt.

They had humbled a symbol of Western Imperialism, something they had so railed against, trampled upon its hallowed grounds, yet, to these soldiers, it meant nothing. They were fighting a war against that which the very Bel Retiro stood for. They had made history, but they were unable to be aware of the gigantic step they had made in the history of mankind. It meant little to them.

When they finally had to ease themselves again, it was not the toilets they used but the grounds outside its gates.

Their duties over, they started down the tracks again, this time seemingly with greater understanding of what they were doing. For they began to sing and when they came into sight again they seemed cheerful and happy even if their voices were not particularly soft and pleasant.

Alamak. Was that all?

But they are not the only faces we see.
We also see the faces of those
With no concern with the war
Over whom wars are fought. Those
Tossed about by the storms of war,
The innocent who suffer in silence
The unimportant whom history will ignore.

9. WHOM HISTORY WILL IGNORE

EVEN before the evacuating ferries reached Singapore, my father had returned from camp where he was on duty as an air raid warden. He seemed exhausted and bitter as he came to Claremont, having walked up the rail tracks in his uniform and still carrying his rifle.

He had a sad tale to relate. He told us how Khoon Teik had returned to camp early that morning, after passing the night in his house when the ship sailed away without him.

It was not because the departure of the British had hurt him. As a matter of act, he was himself trying to sail away. It was the fact that they had left him behind that hurt. They had left him ignorant of what was to happen to him. It was when the actual orders to board the ferries were given and as he was trying to make his way up the gangway that he was told and physically barred from boarding the ferry.

As a senior officer in the legal office, but for his colour, he had every right to expect evacuation, instead of which he had been insulted directly and openly.

My father sympathised with him. His treatment struck a chord in my father. But that was all he could do; that and venting their anger. The least the departing officers could have done was to leave him instructions, as the most senior officer to be left behind, what he should do with the island.

We could not fight on. There was nothing to fight with. Surrender was the only thing we could do unless it was the intention to let the Japanese continue to bomb the island till they physically occupied it.

But the most pressing need was to disband the air-raid wardens and the volunteers, these he and my father decided to do.

By leaving the island in silence, without putting anyone in charge, the people had been let down and left without a leader. I could feel the bitterness and contempt in my father' voice as he spoke and the sun, rising in the sky over our roof, emphasised this by etching the drawn lines on his face.

We relieved him of his rifle and gave him a change of clothes. It was pointless to own any uniform and the rifle would only get him into trouble. We burnt the uniform and buried the rifle in the jungle away from the house.

Swiftly, his pensive mood changed and he grew reflective as he began one of his famous soliloquies, comparing the fatalistic philosophy of the Japanese to that of the egoistic acquisitive nature of the West.

In his view, the outcome of the battle in the north of the country had shown the superiority of the stoic and self-sacrificing nature of the Japanese and their loyalty to their Emperor over the individualist and selfish ego of the West. The Japanese soldier could be called upon to put their duty before themselves. They could be called to sacrifice themselves without question, the British soldiers could not.

That was why they could defeat China, with its corrupt officials and warlords. That was how they had been so effective against the West. They had left Penang in the lurch, those were his favourite words for let down, and he did not believe that they vanished without leaving instructions behind.

It was his opinion which he sometimes seemed to hold. But one could discern a tone of disappointment in his voice of someone who, deep in his heart still had much respect for the British.

For my father was born at the end of the Victorian era at the turn of the 19th century and he had gone to finish his education and to study law in Cambridge in the secure calm just before World War I.

Brought up in a period when the general belief was that the British Empire was one on which the sun would never set, believing in the Victorian era when honour and loyalty were British values, he was of the time of G. Bernard Shaw and the Fabians, when style and dignity were the refinement of thinking, before the world was overtaken by the rough and tumble of ideological wars and to die for King and Country became a joke.

Now he was observing something unpalatable to him. The British had been a great nation and it had a culture and civilisation. It had brought about a system of the supremacy of law and order which had gained recognition throughout nearly half the world.

With it had come decency, respect for democracy and for the rights of others. Notwithstanding that she was still an empirical nation, there was the rule of law. It was not flawless, like everything else. That was to be expected.

Picture the image of an old veteran bemused by a rapid change of events, in an old soldier's uniform, looking at the sky, wondering what was taking place, and feeling that his world had turned upside down and you would have a fair image of him.

Part of him, reflected in the way he had added griffins to a new balcony of his house holding painted shields on which his Cambridge college crest had been painted on, imagining a rapacious army devouring all he had stood for in honour, pride and decency, overthrowing the established in a brutal fashion was something he could not accept.

He had been a tireless critic of British colonialism and the Asian part of him provided for a surreptitious admiration of Japan. But the brutal way it was done, the lack of human respect and decency, the violence with which they had entered the land to destroy everything, was something he could not stomach.

Looking at the quiet desolate sky to the East over the city, one moment stooped in disappointment, drained of all his beliefs, the next moment tightened with uplift by some unknown spirit; he was at once in solace and yet full of vigour and anger and you wonder which is the correct image of him.

As he argued loudly to himself, one could as well see that he had no misunderstanding of the Japanese invasion. It was a new colonialism. The Japanese were no better than the British except that they were out of date by at least a century in their political thinking.

Then, finally, he ended. "Even Jesus," he concluded, "had to bow before Pontius Pilate."

*Even as the sounds of war subside
To the silence of death, the sounds
Of the whimpering take their place
As those still alive try to shake off
The dust of the ruins and the smell
Of a past civilisation shattered,
To retread, with little more than
The slim sinews of hope, a new life
And with unsure and trembling hands,
Rebuild for themselves new homes.*

10. IN DAZED WONDERMENT

WHEN I saw him ready to begin his work at the crack of dawn the next morning, which was his lifetime habit, he had recovered his spirit and was clear as to what he had to do. He was going down to the foot of the hill where the village of Ayer Hitam was. I did not know why he was going down till we reached the foot of the hill when he went directly to the police station there.

The village had become the centre of activity on the island since it was now surrounded by most of the refugees from the city, Georgetown, which stood at the broad promontory to the eastern side of the island. It was now the only place where law and order could emanate and the police station had been evacuated by the police.

However, to my surprise, as my father approached the police station, I could see that it had already been occupied by a small band of armed volunteers and that Lim Khoon Teik, who seemed to be in command, was waiting for him.

It became obvious that even as the volunteers were dismissed, my father had arranged that they should meet there. It explained his uniform and his rifle which he had brought with him. But his rifle was not necessary for it was quickly agreed that my father would be the civil administrator of the village whilst Lim Khoon Teik would be responsible for policing it.

That was how it was when the Japanese authorities came to the village a few days later after the small squad of soldiers had looked over the hill.

The war had terminated a society. In that way it is a death. But with the death there had to come a new beginning and a new structure.

To each his own. I had nothing to do with them. I walked my way to the market behind, following my father after he and Khoon Teik had sorted out who was to do what.

My father had a volunteer escort and he began to bring order to the chaos.

It was strange and a stimulating experience to see volunteers performing the duties of the police and my father taking charge of the situation, drawing lines along the sides of the road and compelling the hawkers to arrange themselves into lines and the householders to queue up and register themselves for rationing.

Leadership had again proved to be a natural result arising from a need. There was also the silent assumption of authority naturally assumed as command was naturally accepted because of a need.

There was something proud in the image of my father walking around the marketplace dispensing law and order in the chaotic aftermath of the fall of the island and the collapse of all authority. His intention was clear and noble enough. But he seemed not to be concerned with the needs of the family. Perhaps he had assumed that my brother and I were there for that purpose. After all, we were already young, if tender, men.

Whatever may have been his thoughts I could not help but admire him and Khoon Teik and those volunteers with him.

But I did not go down the hill to help my father. I had my own plans even if they were not as altruistic as his.

I had ten dollars in my pocket which was all I had in the world and I had determined that with it I would survive the war. I began by helping those up the hill to stock their larders with canned provisions which soon ran out of supply as they were imported from Europe and America.

My intentions were motivated for private as well as for a public purpose. My concern was equally clear but completely opposite to that of my father's.

The market seemed to be a place of frenzy as buyers, their fears of the soldiers forgotten for the moment in their anxiety to stock up, jostled and pushed and almost fell over one another in their hurry to grab whatever they could lay their hands on. Their shouting and screaming rendered it almost impossible to speak normally.

Yet it was only yesterday that they were in panic and almost trampled on one another as they ran for their lives.

The Ayer Itam market was a village market and normally filled with all sorts of produce from the farms and hills. But it was now a huge marketplace, swelled by goods taken from abandoned British warehouses.

The entire village square was crammed full of goods and the noise of women bargaining and shouting confirmed its nature as an Eastern Sunday market rather than a scene of a war. There were puppies, cats, snakes, poultry and such oddities amongst fresh vegetables piled with clothing, pills and drugs for sale without any apparent rule or order.

My interest was in the tinned and bottled provisions and they could be seen everywhere, piled sky high. There were honey, jams, marmalade, sardines and pilchards, luncheon meat, canned potatoes, beetroot, sugar, apples, pears and fruit juices everywhere, no doubt coming from abandoned British warehouses.

The thought that I would probably be buying loot briefly crossed my mind to be dismissed by the argument that it was trivial and since the warehouses had been abandoned, we had as much right as the Japanese to them. Of course, the Japanese disagreed with this argument and they cut off the heads of two youths reportedly caught "looting" in public, at the square of the police headquarters in Penang Road. But that was afterwards.

It was not long before I had exhausted my ten dollars and the basket I was carrying had become quite heavy on my arm. I was soon on my way up the hill to begin a rather lucrative trade and a new life which lasted till the refugees decided to leave the hills and return to their homes a short while later by which time I had become a full-fledged sundry shopkeeper with a small shop behind the police station. Later, I abandoned Ayer Hitam to come back to the city.

I was born in 1922, and was only twenty when all this began. This is not an excuse for any of my wrongdoing, but only to show how much these events could have influenced my thinking. For example, for the first time, I was confronted with a conflict between personal survival and public welfare. What both my father and Khoon Teik did were public duties for the good of society. They exhibited leadership qualities and they were doing it voluntarily to bring order to chaos, maintaining the civil rules of society.

What I was doing was for myself. It made me sensitive to my actions. I had to justify this to myself. My role in the war had little to do with the prosecution of the war either as a defender or a persecutor. My education in practical morality was beginning to be etched on my mind with this conflict.

I could see that man is not only an animal who has to survive for himself but that he is a social animal as well and that he needs to have a responsibility and duty to maintain the health of his society without which he cannot live, for man cannot survive alone.

Taking that argument into the meaning and the reasons for war, I was able also to see that there is as much the expression of the greed and the ambition of man and that some of them foment it as part of the fulfilment of his nature and that the conflict of religion, of morality, loyalties and national beliefs or even ideologies may just be excuses.

I do not think that Japan was justified in going to war. I believe it was the ambition of a few ultra nationalists and the greed of the militarists for power that led Japan to war. In that way, their leaders were accountable internationally if only for the good of the international well-being.

This argument was the beginning of a process in me which would challenge the meaning of loyalty and the moral meaning of war. It also made me relate myself to my society and my role in it, right or wrong.

For the moment, I was in a logjam. I sat down on a root of a forest tree and rested for a while with Ayer Hitam out of sight and below me, hidden by the trees. I was not sure if what I was doing was right. The logjam persisted and I decided to let time unravel it.

Thinking of those up the hill waiting for provisions and for the sulphanilamide MB 125 and 693 pills I had picked up which were as useful as antibiotics (at that time as yet undiscovered) for wounds and injuries during the war and laying aside further argument which seemed niceties and impractical scholastic arguments at such times of survival, I picked up my basket and resumed my laborious journey up the hill, leaving my father and Khoon Teik and their small band of volunteers to their duties. No one had asked for my help.

But, if anyone deserved recognition for acts during the war, it was, as I have suggested, Saravanamuthu and Allan who probably stopped the unnecessary bombing of Penang and Lim Khoon Teik and my father as well as their faithful gang of volunteers who probably started the first self-government of a colony. It is strange how sometimes movements begin in such a peculiar and unheralded manner.

As for myself, of course I deserve nothing. My rewards were in my profits and my survival. No one owed me anything.

*For the living cannot hope to avoid
The future or look back at the dead.
Life continues and nature dictates
That their bridge to the future
Must be found where new leaders
With new promises of hope abound.*

11. THE SINEWS OF HOPE

UNTIL they saw the Japanese soldier, he was a distortion which fear twisted disproportionately. But once he had made an appearance, the reality was easier to cope with.

As for those up the hill, the added realisation that the hill was equally accessible made the itch to return to their homes more difficult to resist and the pressure to return home to the life they were used to irresistible. Like sparrows agitated by the evening light to return home, the women gathered in the kitchens and began to debate the pros and cons of staying on in the darkness of the jungle or returning home to their *mahjong* sessions and opting for the comforts of city life.

Complaints about the strange jungle noises, the absence of streetlights to break the interminable darkness of the nights, the discomfort of unfamiliar and cold pillows, their inability to have a fix when awakened suddenly in almost total darkness and surrounded by the unfamiliar sounds of the jungle and the absence of familiar city noises, they became vociferous for visiting neighbours and friends, and, soon, the exodus back to the city began.

The first to do so was the family of Yeap Chor Ee, with him taking the lead. But for him the reason was not the same. He was the owner of the Ban Hin Lee Bank, one of the banks owned by local owners. He had the keys to the strong room. The Japanese had insisted that all the banks be reopened. They had even recruited the services of locksmiths to force open the vaults of the British banks. He could not refuse to go down to open the vault of his own bank.

But, if they thought they were returning home to their usual life after a picnic, they were sadly mistaken. No sooner had they gone down when the reality of a new life under a new regime struck them. The Japanese were not the neighbours they thought they were.

The city no longer had its familiar noises. The cries of the hawkers could no longer be heard, nor did the ringing of bicycle bells disturb the morning calm. The city had changed. Everything had changed.

Instead, it was filled with strangeness and an absence of gaiety. A strange silence had taken its place. Misgivings began to grow and the reality of the occupation began to sink in.

The astonishing speed of the Japanese army had given no time for the British forces to regroup. Within a week after they had cut through the Jitra Line, they were poised to land on the island.

But the main body of troops did not enter the island. They swept past, anxious to force the British forces as far south as possible before there could be any counter offensive. But a small group was sent in to occupy the island.

As I have said, the behaviour of the occupying troops did not match their prowess on the battlefield. Though their military skill and discipline could not be faulted, the same cannot be said of their occupying troops and their political and civil skills.

There had been no grand or triumphal entry in the style of General George Patton or Douglas MacArthur or the waving of flags. There was no attempt to show any sense of pride and honour of victory. There was only the almost surreptitious landing of a small group of rough and uncultured men in uniform who quickly fanned out from the harbour into the town.

They were rapists as well. The first news of their arrival was followed quickly by news of rape. Rumour had it that there were some five or six such incidents involving young women from good homes. If the incidents were few, the fact that they were perpetrated by only a small squad was enough to create the impression and an image that did not justify their claim that Japan had come to liberate the people from their colonial yoke. It damaged the reputation of Japan irretrievably even when two of the rapists were eventually arrested and taken to account for their crimes in Ipoh where the field headquarters of the Japanese army was established after the fall of Penang.

When the main occupation forces came in, instead of placating the people as psychological warfare required, they began to plunder the town and collect whatever booty they could find, doing exactly what armies had been doing for centuries.

It was all the more distasteful to a Baba-and-Nyonya society which was brought up to respect law and order.

If there was any intention of winning over the people, already in some awe and admiration of them, it was never shown or exploited.

Instead of placating the people and putting them at their ease, they showed at once that they were a rapacious army, uncivilised and uncultured, and demonstrated their lack of awareness at the same time.

They stopped whatever vehicles they could on the road and forcibly took them away. Usable trucks, cars and even motorcycles in their way were taken from their owners by force. If they saw someone driving a car, they would stop the car at bayonet point, pull the occupants roughly out and drive the vehicle away. In that way property disappeared from the possession of their owners, most never to be seen again.

They not only looted but also desecrated homes. Their ordnance corps did not waste time commandeering the best homes for their officers without as much as an acknowledgement or taking an inventory of the contents of these houses or a thank you.

Japan was hungry for the raw materials of war. She needed iron and steel for her war and reparations to help her prosecute the war. The army did not waste time in taking whatever steel they could find even without paying for it and damaging our property.

So it was that the tall and imposing gates of my grandfather's home in Prangin Road, made in Southampton with British iron, failed to stand through the occupation. They were pulled down and broken and taken away. So were the Southampton gates of Chatsworth House, next to us, along the imposing homes of the millionaires in Northam Road, now Jalan Sultan Ahmad Shah.

In fact, all the imposing houses for which Penang was famous, lost their front teeth, so to speak, to the rapacious needs of the Japanese war machine.

Our house, with its less imposing and locally made gates, suffered the same indignity. They had an interesting history. My father had intended to call the house "Hardwicke" after the Lord Chancellor of England. But he did not want one from England and had the gates forged locally as a gesture of defiance to tradition and to strike a blow for independence.

Unfortunately, the local forger was not English-educated and had wrongly forged the name as "Hardwich" so my father had to put on a brave face and resolutely put up the gates with the wrong spelling as if he had intended it from the beginning.

My most important personal concern were the two volumes of "The Wonders of Animal Life" which I had assiduously compiled out of a weekly magazine as a schoolboy. It had taken a great deal of patience and I was proud of what I had done. The first thing when I went home was to go to the drawer where I had kept them. The Japanese troops had been through the house. The gasters were missing and the doors had been left open and my volumes were not there. Someone had taken them away though they would have meant little to him. Imagine my disappointment and disgust. To me, the loss was even greater than the loss of our gates.

It was not so much the fact that they did what they had to do but the way they did it that made them uncouth and unworthy of their own claim as liberators of Southeast Asia. In fact, when they first entered the peninsula, those who had never accepted British sovereignty welcomed them in their Friday best, but they, as well as the freedom fighters who thought they would be on the same side, turned against them, disenchanted by the way they behaved.

Japan did not mean what she had portrayed. The Japanese army was no respecter of other peoples' rights, history or pride. Their troops were not fighting a liberation war but a primitive war with modern weapons and machines. The individual soldier was also a feudal peasant, politically unequal to his task and his ill-mannered behaviour emptied the streets as the people hid themselves in terror. Nor did they bother to keep the city clean. That was their last priority. The mess of the bombing was left there, with the blood, till the rains came. Nor did they bother to remove the rubble or clear up the mess.

Such then was the state of the silent city when the refugees finally returned to them. Instead of returning to the state of affairs they had been accustomed to, they were met with resounding slaps by sentries because they did not bow to them and, to add insult to injury, it was a common sight to see soldiers unbuttoning their trousers everywhere, mostly along roadsides, peeing willy-nilly and farting openly.

What is war but pillage and rape, and
The lowly musty smell of sweat and fear?
Who understands, even amongst the victors,
War's noble motives and high ideals
Who have fought to kill and die?

12. WHIMPERING FACES

IT was difficult to imagine what could be worse than the *Kempeitai*. We had never seen anything so deliberately brutal and crude. It was as if terror had been turned into a system and an art.

Since it was also a military police force which dealt with political crimes, one expected them to be more educated than the ordinary soldier. For they were not peasants but selected personnel with more awareness and education for the job they were doing. Yet they behaved with unexplainable savagery that one could only assume that, for a nation with so much professed culture, this was surprising unless one took their systematic cruelty to be also a culture they had developed.

They came in with the first occupation troops. As soon as they had landed on the island, they immediately displayed their cold and ruthless efficiency. Armed with lists of wanted people and their addresses provided by their agents posing as photographers and dentists before the war, accompanied by some of the very same people who could be recognised, they went straight to the homes of known anti-Japanese elements to exterminate them.

How many were taken away and shot I do not know for they did everything in secrecy. But their two main targets, the leaders of the Aid China Campaign managed to avoid capture.

The Aid China Campaign was a spontaneous movement resulting from popular sentiment of overseas Chinese that they should help their motherland. It was not a political movement because it was spontaneous and arose out of a popular emotional background. All it did was to raise funds and to arrange for volunteers to drive trucks across Burma to China with aid. But the Japanese *Kempeitai* considered these to be acts of treachery which they avenged with savagery.

One of the two was Ong Kheng Seng, a prominent Chinese society leader. The other was Lau Geok Swee, with a more political bent.

It was fortunate that Ong Kheng Seng passed away just before the outbreak of the war. Lau Geok Swee had business interests in Sumatra and he slipped away in one of his junks just before they came and he remained in Sumatra for the duration of the war.

But the *Kempeitai* had other victims to catch and they concentrated their efforts on the students of Chinese schools known for their anti-Japanese activities, rounding up and cordoning off streets in their sweeping searches for these young men, many of whom escaped the dragnet by skipping off to other homes and to anti-Japanese fringe areas where they were not known and where such sweeps could not be effective. Those caught were simply spirited away and never returned.

An incident which happened a few days into the occupation would give one an idea of their ruthlessness and disregard for human lives. Two youths were apparently caught "looting" from abandoned British warehouses. We do not know if the warehouses had been thrown open to the public or if one of them had been broken into by the two youths. There was not even a semblance of a trial. They were executed in Japanese style.

Since the Japanese themselves openly looted the town and never paid for the goods they took away (including driving away cars and tearing down iron gates that did not belong to them), cutting off the heads of these two youths in public without even a show trial seemed a bit too much. What the two youths did exactly, we will never know.

All that notwithstanding, the two youths, blindfolded and with hands tied behind their back, were brought out to the square of the police headquarters in Penang Road (then the main thoroughfare of the city) for their execution.

Passersby were diverted into the square by soldiers and when there were enough onlookers, a Japanese officer stepped up to the youths and one after the other was made them to kneel in the square. In swift succession, he cut off their heads, swiping his blade after each execution with a piece of cloth even as his victims were still kicking on the ground, and looking at the crowds each time as he cleaned his sword as if to force home the message of the *Kempeitai*.

I was not there. I was spared the sight of this inhumanity. But, in the eyes of one of the beholders, "the blood just gushed out like a fountain when the sword went down and their legs jerked back as the sword struck!" These were not the words of any sophisticated person but those of a simple maid in her teens from the household who had excitedly taken leave to watch the execution when she heard someone saying that there would be one that morning.

The heads of the executed youths were not exhibited but the executions had a salutary effect. The island was practically crime free for the duration of the war and there were no burglaries at all and the people could just leave their homes unattended and their doors unbolted. But did the punishment fit the crime? For all that effectiveness, was it justified and not a totalitarian act?

The dark shadow of the *Kempeitai* hung over the city like an ever present nightmare. They had the power to take whatever action they pleased and they seemed to be purely acting out their nature. The best that can be said for them is that at least they acted summarily and brutally and they did not act like cats playing with mice.

Responsibility could be guilt by association and their enforcing instrument for such crime was torture till the information they wanted to hear was extracted from the prisoner or he died in the torture.

Mass execution was another form of punishment where ten persons would be taken out and executed for every Japanese soldier killed. Fortunately for us, unlike in Singapore and elsewhere, such killings did not occur in Penang.

Fortunately for us, in the case of Sir Gerald Templer, who was to employ similar tactics in his fight against Communism during the period of the Malayan Emergency between 1948 and 1960, did not employ the extreme punishment. Even so, the people were put behind barbed-wire villages and food was rationed and controlled.

But he was accountable to public opinion in England, though it was far away, and the punishments were made in full view of the press and its criticism. In the case of the *Kempeitai*, they seemed accountable to no one till the war-crime hearings when much of the evidence had been destroyed and the identities of the perpetrators lost.

It would be interesting to speculate how things would turned out had the *Kempeitai* been more astute, kind, polite and considerate. But that is doubtful and remains pure speculation. If the comfort home was a moral horror on which there can be some argument, the *Kempeitai* was without argument, a horror with or without moral argument.

The mass sweeps by cordoning off areas to take out suspects, were carried on throughout the most part of the war. We called it a "roundup".

It was usually done just before dawn when the Japanese police would cordon off a block of a few streets.

That done, a few soldiers accompanied by detectives would go from house to house, waking up the inmates whose young and able-bodied males would be made to stand in the street outside their homes in single file on both sides of the street.

Then, after what seemed like hours, an open truck would come down the street slowly with hooded men inside who would identify anyone they wanted by a nod in his direction. The few soldiers accompanying the truck would then reach out and grab the man and throw him inside a prison van (accompanying the truck) amidst the protest and weeping of women. The unfortunate victim would never know the identity of the hooded men or whether they were detectives, informers or just prisoners who were promised a false freedom if they betrayed their friends.

This procession of hooded men would slowly move down the street followed by the prison vans till they reached the other end of the street when they would speed off with the men they had picked up never to be seen again.

Such roundups were frequent at the beginning of the occupation and it was a guessing game as to who would be picked up, since anyone could be picked up as a result of a grudge or for the look on his face. The rumour was always that those taken away would be shot and buried in mass graves. The suspense was always intense and women had been known to have fainted under that pressure for no one ever knew if a loved one would be the next victim.

Nor have any of the rumoured mass graves ever been publicly discovered or the human remains in them ever declared or identified.

I was once nearly caught in one of such roundups. Early one morning, even before dawn had pierced the sky, we were awakened by the strange barking of dogs. I don't know if you have ever heard the barking of dogs in a strange and threatening environment. Either the dogs sensed that there was some strange impending danger or I was imagining. But I heard barks that had a sort of whining mixed with it.

Having heard roundups from the earliest days of the occupation and suspicious of the barking, I cautiously looked out of the window and found some soldiers almost at our door.

I was lucky that I had chosen to stay in a house with a back lane that led to other back lanes and out to Macalister Road next to the mosque where Dr Ong Chong Keng had a house at the corner. I knew him and would go round to see him in the evenings for he would go to the house at nights after dinner to learn about public speaking and how he viewed politics. I still remember he told me he would spend ten minutes every morning in his toilet memorising and honing a speech he had prepared two months before delivery. I remember how he emphasised on delivery and language for effect and being struck by the fact that politicians in his time were less interested in causes as impressions.

I therefore knew how to get to his house even during curfew time. That morning, this knowledge and preparation stood me in good stead.

We all knew what a roundup was and this was obviously one, and we were already nearly too late. Peering out of the window in the half light, I could see figures knocking at doors nearly opposite. In no time at all, they would be at our door and any sound suggesting flight would certainly be met with immediate military reaction.

There was little time. Telling the maid to straighten out the bed-sheets and to shut the back door after us before going back to bed and pretending to sleep, my wife and I got hold of our bicycles and in no time at all were out of the house, pedalling as fast as we could down the back lane into safety. I was lucky; I was never caught again in a roundup.

The *Kempeitai* were not wrong to concentrate their efforts on students of the Chinese schools. The students of the English schools were Empire and not China orientated. They knew little of Chinese affairs and were therefore generally not dangerous, and, unless something went wrong or they were mistakenly taken away in a roundup, the Japanese were not interested in them.

It was a different matter with the students of the Chinese schools who were politically pro-China and therefore anti-Japanese. But how politically committed they were we would never know for the activities and the persistent efforts of the Japanese to look for enemy agents within their ranks automatically made them enemies.

They were divided into the Kuomintang and the Pro-Communist groups with the latter more recalcitrant and indoctrinated. Here the Japanese and the British had common foes and therefore they could use the same Special Branch as did the British. They therefore had the advantage of the Special Branch files and the personnel of the Special Branch which they exploited. All one heard were screams and cries emanating from places of interrogation in the early period of the occupation.

Nor did they really distinguish between them in their treatment of them once it was found that they were hostile to the Japanese. That is not saying much, for few Chinese were not hostile. But the Kuomintang (or the Nationalists) were not revolutionaries, they were pro-government for they were pro-Chiang Kai Shek. Their organisation was therefore less clandestine in nature and structure and so they fell easy victims to the Japanese.

But the Left was clandestine in nature and structure. They therefore knew the routes into the jungle and the friendly jungle fringes. They were thus to form an anti-Japanese army in the jungle which was subversive and aggressive even if it was not so effective. They set up the support groups which could succour and feed them.

It was on such that the Japanese were at their worst. One heard of bamboo slivers being driven under their nails, of the water treatment where water was pumped in and then stamped out of their stomachs, of suspending them from pillars by their hands tied behind their backs, and in one reported case of a young communist suspect being tied by her breasts to the tread of a motorcycle and dragged around the prison courtyard for her to give information of her comrades and how she eventually died for refusing to open her mouth—perhaps she did not have anything to tell, who knows?

They were so strange that it is quite believable that no one but a pervert or a sadist could have worked as a *Kempeitai*. The organisation seemed to attract such persons. The chief of the Penang *Kempeitai*, Suzuki, for example, seemed such a person. Of extreme sensitivity and talent, he played Bach quietly into the evenings and one sometimes heard him play. Yet he was known to have caught a young Indian boy stealing at the wharf in Butterworth and it seemed that he took the boy to the pier and decapitated him there, kicking his body into the sea. He could be heard sometimes playing Bach on the piano in his home next to the Methodist Church in Burmah Road where he had set up the *Kempeitai* headquarters and its interrogation rooms where screams and cries of pain often could be heard in the evenings.

Hard, hard, hard are victorious eyes
As they burn with cold, cold gaze
Into the glazed eyes of the tortured.

Hard, hard, hard are the faces that
Gaze, eyeball to eyeball, upon
Glazed eyes of the dying and the dead.

13. HARD ARE THE FACES

THE Japanese comfort home is another example of the crudity and the primitive way the Japanese militarists viewed human life, especially the human lives of non-Japanese. Their argument for their existence was that the natural urge of youths had to be satisfied and that this was better than to let them run all over town at risk to themselves and the safety of innocent girls. That they considered rape an atrocity was clear by the way they took immediate action against the perpetrators in the early days of the occupation. It was also true that no reprisals were taken.

All that is true enough. After all we have the seduction at Western bars in Europe and the R&R escapades during the Korean and Vietnam wars, both of which are unsavoury.

But if true, the Japanese way was compulsive and crude and it was the unpleasant way things were done that made the case against them, even if no force was used which was not always the case.

Even as the troops were advancing from Jitra, the rumour that the pregnant wife of an English planter had been raped and quartered and that her dismembered parts had been stuck to the four ends of the Sungei Patani bridge had preceded them.

No one was interested in verifying that tale or if there were English planters north of Penang at all. Such stories were salacious and tempting to repeat and so the Japanese soon gained a reputation for their cruelty.

To Chinese women at that time whose virginity no dowry could ever recompense, this was a fate worse than death. Is it then a surprise that young Chinese women began to wear their hair short to pass off as young men with the aid of their brothers' clothes?

And it is not surprising if many a young girl heaved a sigh of relief when the comfort homes were established and housed by others. To them, to be taken into a comfort home was a fate worse than death; to the Japanese military it was patriotic duty in the service of their motherland that they should service the gallant young soldiers.

The arguments on both sides could not have been more straightforward. But the serious flaw of the Japanese argument which they could not see, was that they were applying that argument to foreign women whom they conquered, not their own women. Though sex was a natural thing, it did not occur to them that the way it was satisfied was as important as the fact that it had to be satisfied. To them, they were the victors and victors took what they wanted.

Their social mores were different and crude. They were not even values they would apply to their own women. But they saw nothing wrong in the way foreign women were used. "Used" was the exact term in this instance because we are dealing with feudal minds.

The brothel, or the *geisha*, or the "tea houses" was an eastern tradition, as can be read in the *Golden Lotus*, the *Dream of the Red Chamber* and *The Scholar*, all of them Chinese classics. The flaw in such argument was that they were applying a feudal argument to a modern era and that they applied this argument on the victims of war unable to resist them.

Fortunately, there was something else that applied to Penang which came into the equation which saved many from embarrassment. Penang was a sea port town well known for its professionals before the war. So, when the need came, these women saved the day and they were used to serve the homes.

When news came that women had been found for these homes, it was greeted with immense relief by many a young girl and their parents who were not so concerned with morality as with the safety of their own children and themselves.

They were not about to make a song and dance about the rights of the prostitute. Faced with a situation where a solution had to be found which would satisfy the soldier and leave their honour intact, nothing could be further from their minds.

If all this does not make moral sense, it at least made logical sense. Such is the curse of war. Nor did the question of how or how much coercion had to be imposed upon those women before they agreed to fill the comfort homes concern them. It was a nicety few of the nice girls were concerned with. Professionals were not regarded with high esteem nor was morality really an issue but only the exigency of the dire circumstances. If sex could not be avoided, at least the decent, especially the virgin, should be saved.

I knew of two men responsible for part of this relief. One was the brother of a schoolteacher who was the manager of a dance hall before the war. His argument was simple. He could not see why the young girls should have been forced if he could fill those homes with Penang's seaport prostitutes even if he had been something of a pimp. Let us not be hypocrites, he argued. These girls were already earning their living in this way and there was no reason to assume that they would not want to continue their trade. Do you want your friends to be abducted? He asked. I really could not answer him. He was convinced he was morally right.

The other had much the same argument. He was a rice trader before the war and he thought in terms of a trader. His reason might have been more profit inclined but he maintained he had chosen to do the lesser of two evils. That it certainly was.

There would come a time, just after reoccupation, when a few men had taken the liberty to shave the heads of some women for fraternising with the enemy; but not for prostitution. Indeed, there was fraternising and there was resentment, but I know of no case where inmates of these homes suffered such indignities.

I could never have envisaged the comfort homes had I not myself come across them during the war. Nor could I have thought of romance for a fee. Such a thing was abhorrent. It was difficult for me to imagine that women could enjoy themselves in such a situation.

Can you imagine my surprise when I subsequently heard and saw what was going on in a comfort home? From the laughter and gaiety I saw and heard, I found it difficult to believe that any of those women had been forced. It did not make me easy or proud, coming from an occupied territory. But it made me think.

These were prostitutes and there was no reason why they should stop plying their trade and their support. If the reason for them was economic hardship, the situation had not changed during the Japanese regime.

It was in the evening when I came upon this scene. The trishaws were busy plying their trade, taking many a pretty woman, all dressed up in their finery and seemingly happy and smiling as they were being taken to a home. I was to see the same thing after the war in Taipei where women were taken by their boyfriends to the official comfort homes of Taiwan. It is difficult to throw stones at the Japanese by those living in glasshouses.

The other day I spoke to a retired officer of the state to find out his views on the subject. I told him what I thought of the whole thing I was about to put on paper and was surprised to find him in agreement with me. Whilst one cannot forgive compulsion, he did not find any. As a small boy, he told me, he used to go along the river bank at Prai in the evenings at low tide to look for crabs. The number of discarded condoms (then called "french letters") by the river bank astounded him.

There was a comfort home nearby, he explained. And as he went by he would often hear peals of laughter and giggling coming through the quiet of the twilight from this home and I wondered what the moral protesters of today would have done under the circumstances that existed during the occupation in front of the thousands of Japanese troops with a different sense of morality to theirs.

How then did this matter become such a large indignant issue today? Obviously the main reason was because force was used. But there is another more subtle and pervasive reason and that is the psychological reaction one has towards sexual matters. Few can take sex of others objectively. To this has been added the confusion of the various attitudes taken by different beliefs.

G. Bernard Shaw has argued that morality is a middle-class idea. But Bernard Shaw was talking of morality generally. Applied specifically to sex, to this confusion are the different attitudes to sex by the different civilisations and religious and other beliefs.

I have said that the roots of the comfort homes can be found in Chinese sources. Let me elaborate.

The Chinese belief was that sex cannot be related to marriage and family. It was something found outside the home and it did not affect family relationships which were taken to have been arranged according to the fates. The tea houses were places of entertainment from which mistresses could sometimes be found as was shown in the *Golden Lotus* and the other romances of the Chinese manner.

The *geisha* homes were the Japanese equivalent but with greater refinement where trained artisans entertained guests to dinner. I had never been to one and I was anxious to discover if I was right but I did not have a chance to find this out until some time in the 1960s when a friend of my sister, Fumio, in the United States to studying advertising and public relations, wrote to his father, a judge in Japan to show me one.

No doubt the comfort home was a corruption, or a debased version, of it. But I was introduced to the modern Chinese version of the tea house early in the war which gave me a measure with which to compare the comfort home.

Soon after the Eposho was formed, in the very early days of the war, I conceived the excuse of taking a consignment of tinned curry to Singapore for sale. Merchants had legitimate reason for travelling and I was of the age where such a reason might be one that stood between life and death as I would have to pass through the peninsula and the Japanese were still actively looking for Communist "terrorists".

There was no news from Singapore and my intention was not really to sell anything but to satisfy my curiosity to see how my College friends in Singapore had fared in the war and the collapse of Singapore where there had been an active defence by the local inhabitants.

At the conclusion of the sale which took place the day after our journey which I had undertaken with a Teochew partner, Cho Suan, that very morning, we were entertained that evening in the best traditions of Chinese merchants, to dinner at a special Teochew restaurant in Chinatown exclusively catering to known Teochew traders and little frequented by members of the general public.

I am English-educated, without such tradition, and it was my first ever experience in a truly Chinese restaurant and it was an eye-opener as I did not know that there was such elaboration of good manners. I somehow felt rather privileged to be taken to that dinner. It was, to me, an insight into a citadel of Chinese culture.

The dinner took place in a small hall of a small building with room only for about three or four tables but our table was the only one occupied. This took place regularly enough with our host, one or two of his friends and a few members of his more important staff.

The food was Teochew and not the usual Cantonese ones we were used to having. As a consequence, I missed the more subtle nuances of its taste. But, looking at the dishes, one would hardly think there was a war on. It was so exotic.

What was the highlight of the evening was after our host silently disappeared towards the end of the dinner and when a little later on, a little man came in and whispered in the ear of my friend to follow him.

By then the dinner was coming to an end and, saying goodnight to those beside us, my friend rose from the table and signalled to me to follow suit, leaving those at the table to conclude their meal.

We were taken upstairs through a creaky staircase to the closed door of a room just after the staircase. I am not sure if this was a small inn of a hotel or merely a small club with a few rooms.

As my friend gingerly opened the door, a strong whiff of a sweet aromatic smell reached my nose; a redolent enticing smell, so distinctive that it immediately reminded me of my uncle who was an opium smoker.

Our host was lying on a broad, low Chinese wooden opium smoker's bed on the far side of the room smoking a pipe. His eyes were already glazed but he had enough consciousness to notice us and to signal us to the empty side of the bed.

In the middle of the bed was a small opium lamp with a glass funnel with huge lips on which opium could be toasted before shaking. A girl, hardly more than fifteen, was sitting beside the lamp in the process of toasting a swab of raw opium on the lips of the lamp when we went in and it accounted for the aroma which flooded the room and wafted to our noses.

As the door was quietly closed behind us, my friend signalled me to sit on a chair by the door and quietly crept across the small room to occupy the empty space on the other side of the bed across our host.

He was soon lying down facing our host, as if a practised smoker, the faint light of the small opium lamp playing on the apparent contentment on his face as he waited for his turn with the opium pipe.

I sat on the chair looking at the girl as she prepared the opium and passed the pipe to my friend, her face passive and inscrutable.

After a puff, for that was what one could do to each swab of opium, my friend handed the pipe back to the girl who then passed it back to the host after preparing yet another swab of opium. The room was full of fragrance and I cannot say I disliked the smell. It is easy to succumb to the smell of opium.

But my friend was experienced. Either he took the trouble not to inhale too much or he did not quite pull at the pipe, I do not know. For he did not succumb to the fumes and when it was obvious that our host was completely lost to the world, he quietly rose to his feet and we both left the room, his opium dreams and the little girl to our host.

My friend had little to say about the opium except that he had to oblige our host and that he did not smoke it. As for the little girl, he seemed to have taken her for granted as no doubt he too had never had anything to say about the comfort homes.

But I did wonder how a young girl like her had come to that situation. And she looked already experienced and practised. Yet she was too young to know what she was doing. She was only part of our culture even if it was economic necessity which had put her into her position.

A person overcome by opium is not concerned with anything but his dreams. She would have an easy time after we left. But there was no doubt that sex was part of her duties.

But to our culture had come opium. It was strange how opium, introduced into China only in the Opium War of the mid-19th century by the British, had also become part of this culture. The brothel was part of this scene, as I have said before, depicted in the Chinese novels such as the *Golden Lotus* and *The After Midnight Scholar*, and it still remains part of Chinese life.

How was this different from the Japanese *geisha*? In a less cultured way? Perhaps that was how Cho Suan understood the *geisha*, accepting the compulsion as a necessary part of the evil of war?

And how does one become a prostitute? One evening, towards the end of the war, a group of young friends thought to celebrate hints of the turning tide of war. There were no such places as places of entertainment during the war. But one could quietly go for a dinner at one of the small hotels in Chulia Street and order a bowl of pork broth and a bit of liquor.

After a while we went into a small room where a young woman came in. Someone must have asked for her. The rest then left the room to me and her. I began speaking to her.

We used a small room in the hotel. As our drinks progressed apace, a young woman, not much older than that opium girl in Singapore, entered the room. To my surprise and sudden realisation, I was alone in the room with her, my other friends, had for some reason or other excused themselves.

It was almost the same scenario as that of my Singapore experience. But instead of the opium bed, there was a bed in a corner of the room and a round Chinese table in the middle of this rather huge and empty room.

I realised what had happened. I had been deliberately left alone in the room to see what I would do. Nevertheless, I was not put off. I was rather intrigued by this girl and even more so when she told me she was hardly sixteen and had a child from her marriage.

My curiosity aroused, I thought to pursue the subject further. If she was married and with a child, what was she doing in the hotel that night.

She was unashamed and forthright and her story was amazing in the way the fates play tricks on the innocents.

She had married young because of the Occupation. Her husband was a sundry shopkeeper in Ayer Hitam where her home was. Her husband had thought to go to Burma in a Chinese junk in his efforts to start an import trade. He had been most unfortunate. It was his first venture and his boat, on its return had met with a British marauding submarine on patrol just off the Andaman islands.

No one could fail to distinguish a Chinese junk with its unmistakable shape. It was a sailing boat of a singular shape and design. It was certainly no warship but the submarine had surfaced and deliberately shelled it to bits. One had to presume she was sunk because the submarine had thought to blockade the island.

Her husband could not swim and was drowned. A returning sailor had given her the bad news and there she was, trying to sell all that she had left to sell, herself.

Since I was a wholesaler, I therefore asked her husband's name. His name did not ring a bell. But when she told me the name of his shop I suddenly thought I knew the man. Did he have a gold tooth? Wasn't he quite a short man in his early twenties? Did he ride a bicycle?

All the answers were in the affirmative, could I be talking about a friend?

My God, I knew him! He was one of the customers of Kean Swee, my import and wholesale company. He used to come to town in the late morning, buy all the goods he wanted and then take delivery and set off home in the afternoon, usually at about three in the afternoon.

I suppose I should have been thunderstruck, but somehow I was only aware of the ghastly truth of talking to a prostitute who was the wife of someone I knew! Why are you here? My questions had come almost involuntarily, as if in the hope of refutation of my fears and not by way of moral indignation. How can one be indignant when facing a truth and an inevitability. If anyone could be blamed, would that not be the captain of the submarine? She was for sale for the night. She was for sale because fate had dealt her an unkind blow. Again, morality had to take a back seat.

I gave her $300 I had on me and told her to go home. What she did the night after I do not know as I never saw her again.

No sooner had she left the room when my friends sheepishly returned. The reason for their absence was immediately disclosed. They had gone upstairs to peep through cracks on the floorboards to see what would take place. Fortunately nothing did take place that they wanted to see and if it was sex, I do not think mine has anything to do with the public.

If my friends were not interested in the strange happenings to a little girl, at least that evening very much affected my judgement and my entire approach to the meaning of war and the moral questions it throws up. Only when we ourselves have been affected by the situation can we care enough to think about it. One should be careful when one casts stones if one lives in a glasshouse.

A more pleasant version of this culture I had observed in Korea. I had gone to Korea and was fortunate enough to be invited to lunch by a senator who had discovered my presence there through a mutual friend who was an antique dealer.

From the expensive look of the restaurant and its sprawling nature it was obvious that it was not a run of the mill sort of place but an exclusive traditional restaurant in which we were served a traditional Korean lunch.

To my surprise it was more Japanese than Chinese and we had to sit on the floor mat around a low square table and we were served by a woman dressed in a Korean *kimono*. Years under Japanese rule had great influence on the Koreans whose rough and insensitive manners are well known throughout the world.

The only difference between the Japanese way of service and the way we were served was perhaps only in the style. The Japanese manner is polite without subservience. The Korean was to me obsequious and polite only in the subservient manner expected from such women.

She came in with the food and, sitting down beside us, she began to prepare it and serve us, speaking in nothing but Korean to our host.

Service here had to be explained. The food came in small dishes and was already prepared to be served. All she had to do was to take up the food with a pair of chopsticks and put it to our mouths, something I could easily do myself. But no, she had to do it.

Fortunately, she used our chopsticks to serve us, his for him and mine for me. All I had to do was to open and shut my mouth and eat my food like I was incapable of doing it myself. I was not used to it and it was embarrassing. I did not want to upset my host and so suffered this indignity throughout the meal, not understanding a word of what she was saying and she knowing that I did not understand.

When lunch was over, she wiped my face with a napkin, collected the dishes and placed them together and, after a few words with our host, rose from the table and disappeared the way she came, out of a door.

It was feudal in the way I was treated and undignified in the way she was treated. She did not have the dignity accorded to the Japanese *geisha* in Japan. Obviously the tradition had originated from China but its equivalent had died out in China long ago. It was a result of Japanese influence and it had developed a closer affinity to the Japanese tradition, Korea having been colonised by Japan. However, Japanese refinement had been brutalised by the way Japan had treated Korea and one could see little of the tastefulness and courtesy one found in Japan. There was a pervading crudity. Even if she was treated as a courtesan there would have at least been a veneer of appreciation of an art.

The time came when I was to see the real *geisha* for myself that would explain the brothel in it finest form even if one could object to the feudal attitude towards women. Fumio was a friend of my sister's family. He came from a respectable family in Japan and his father was a judge which, in Japan, meant that he was a scholar from one of the highest universities of Japan where he had graduated with honours. He would, I presume, have also come from an established and respected family.

Fumio knew I was interested in the origins of the comfort home, and when I met him, thought I should visit his father on my way home to Penang where I was scheduled to handle a murder case.

I briefly stopped over in Japan on my way home and was invited to dinner with him. He gave me an address and told me how to get there. Again, it was a special restaurant that served in a traditional Japanese way. He knew little English but enough for us to meet and speak to each other without intermediaries and in privacy.

The restaurant was tastefully planned and dinner was served in a private room where there was only one low table and cushions over *tatami* mats. I have to admit the Japanese have a good sense of balance and there is a lack of vulgarity one sees in a Chinese restaurant where one is supposed to shout to be heard and loudness is taken for popularity and good patronage.

The impression was a restrained atmosphere and the dinner was typically Japanese and tastefully served by a very pretty and well dressed Japanese *geisha*. I do not know if it is a *geisha* house or not but nowhere else have I ever been served in that manner.

When she came in to serve, she bowed to us as soon as she entered the room before she did anything else, her collected manner and her silk *kimono* and her presence filling the room immediately. With my still fresh impression of the *geisha* I had met when crossing the junction of a street on my way to the restaurant, I could not help thinking that *geishas* were the most well dressed and collected young women in the world. Her attitude and decorum were nice to the extreme.

But, on closer look, the womanly poise and the controlled manners of the *geisha* in front of me were not the natural attributes of youth. She was in her early thirties and her manners were the cultivated discipline of years of training. Her beauty was that of the cultivated kind.

The best *geishas* were not the very young ones but the young ones whose attributes had been discovered when very young and then honed and polished for years. Our *geisha*, he explained, had brought her *samisen* with her and she was an accomplished singer. I chose to take his word for it.

She prepared the food and the *sake* and asked us to help ourselves with the food whilst she served the *sake*.

When we got too involved with our conversation, she would indicate that the food was getting cold. But the service was not obsequious. It was quiet, tasteful and polite. She did not put any food in my mouth. She prepared the food and placed it on our plates and we helped ourselves.

After the dinner, she rose from the table and went a little way away and picked up her samisen and asked if we wanted her to sing. It was obvious that things had been arranged for me to experience something that was the culture of the elite of Japan. I was no elite and I was not interested in someone singing for me during my meal. I thought the singing was not necessary and the *geisha* was dismissed and she withdrew from the room with her back to the door so as not to offend us. It was the *geisha* tradition at its best.

The worst was the comfort home to which my thoughts returned. No one in his sane moments could compare it to the *geisha* house nor any of the inmates to the *geisha* leaving the room.

Let us make no mistake about it. No one in his sane moments would exploit others with so much force and compulsion. But this was war and it dealt with the lives and the sensitivities of the human life of women in occupied lands and both their lives and their sensitivities were expendable.

The Japanese leadership was not much concerned with human lives, especially those in enemy lands. They were not on a picnic. Thousands had just been shot purely in revenge when they overcame Singapore. Thousands would soon be sent to the Death Railway in Burma. The exploitation of women sexually with callous indifference and insensitivity to the feelings of others could hardly be of concern to them.

In fact, on closer examination of the comfort homes, their concern was with the safety of their soldiers more than anything else. Rather than allowing them to take the risk of running around the town at night it was better to collect the women and put them in homes where they could be examined for diseases and their soldiers made secure from risks.

The comfort home was not a debased form of the *geisha* house. It was no more than a brothel and it was used as such. Whether their existence is justified, one cannot agree with the so called psychological school and argue that it was justified as it satisfied a natural desire. That is mere hogwash. One does not fulfil a desire to cure a desire, nor does one cure greed by giving way to it. It only breeds more greed and can become a bad habit.

As for the argument that such things are only natural, we have to remember that many things are natural and that natural things are not always complementary and often contradictory.

No, the comfort homes were established for the benefit of the Japanese and came about because of callousness and insensitivity to the feelings of others. Nor did they attempt to disguise their intention as did the R&R centres later on. That was their crime.

As for the citizens, it was but part of a bad dream. For we had the Kempeitai to think of, survival for one another, safety for ourselves and for members of our immediate families. We had no time really for the niceties of argument and philosophy and, yes, even morality which did not immediately concern us. And, even if we did, there was not enough trust for those around us for us to disclose our true feelings.

The comfort home was an exploitation and any exploitation is bad. But it was only one of the exploitations of war. It left a nasty taste in the mouth that set the tone of the occupation but it was just another face of war.

I shifted my look from the *geisha* to the host who, in the meantime had taken out a piece of paper and was writing on it. He was in a mood to write and he looked serious and kindly.

As he wrote my mind went back again and again to the comfort homes. At long last, I had seen the many versions of sexual entertainment in the world and in Asia. I can only conclude that we do consider sex as something outside of the family—and decency. We are prepared to be indecent outside the home and would not allow what we did to affect the home. This was not the same in the West. Sex and love and family were part and parcel of the entire relationship and the act of any one of those can destroy the rest. What should the solution be?

As I was reflecting, the judge finished what he was writing. What he wrote was simple, his calligraphy educated, firm, full of confidence, sure and fluid. That was the style of entertainment of the literati.

He wrote only sixteen words in all, in groups of four. It was a famous poem, one known to all Chinese and Japanese scholars. The way the evening's entertainment had proceeded, the *geisha* and the writing added to its elegance and beauty.

I knew no Japanese. But the characters of that writing was in the common *kanji* which everyone in Asia who knew Chinese characters could easily understand. In fact, it is a well-known poem.

He folded the writing after he had finished it and handed it over to me with both hands. I received it with both hands. He stood up and bowed to me and I returned the compliment. Actually, I should have bowed first, as he was the elder and more important man.

The poem said: "I have travelled the world and I have seen many things and many people and I find that, throughout the four seas, all men are brothers."

Indeed, all men are brothers. But why do we continue to do what we do to our brothers and sisters? Is that also a natural desire and to which we must give in?

A Persian poem has it that when one part of the body is in pain, the whole body suffers. How is it then that we do not feel the pain in the bodies of our brethren?

I knew that Fumio's father had entertained me for a purpose which had now been made clear in his writing. When we said our final goodbyes outside the restaurant, nothing had been resolved despite the paper. The comfort home still remained a comfort home. It was exploitation of sex by the stronger of the weaker to satisfy a primitive instinct, a trick of nature for the propagation of the race. Whether it be in Europe, China or elsewhere, we have to accept that exploitation, not only of sex, is nevertheless exploitation, and war is the instrument for it, for actually, all these happen as a result of war. It is our biggest nightmare which could one day even end our entire civilisation.

But one thing is also certain, we, who also live in glasshouses must not throw stones. Over twenty years have passed since the last war and still those atrocities are being committed. The actors have changed but the play still goes on. Will it ever stop without clear international will and as long as the culture of war remains?

Blood, blood everywhere
And not a tiny drop is theirs.

Don't sound the trumpets,
The dead cannot hear
The victors are too drunk
And the maimed and injured
Find the sounds too painful.

The victorious are full of dictates,
The defeated can only whimper,
The damned are muted, bereft of curses,
Choked with awareness of death.

14. NOT A TINY DROP IS THEIRS

WHEN the British surrendered in Singapore, it was reputed that a Malay officer was used for bayonet practice because he had done his duty and had resisted the Japanese and some 2,000 local volunteers, almost entirely Chinese, were decimated on the beaches of Changi for doing the same thing. According to Ian Morrison, there were then only 422,000 Chinese in Singapore.

Thus, the Japanese military made it clear from the very beginning their determination to subdue all to their will and their contempt for international sentiment. In that way, too, they had put to a stop the lies their own propaganda machined had made that they had come to liberate the people from the yoke of British imperialism.

Not only were they unaware of the sweeping changes that had come to political thinking in the 20th century but they must have been completely or seemed unaware of the political sensitivities of the people they claimed they had come to liberate.

In the few weeks of victory after victory when they had gained the admiration of the Southeast Asian people, to whom their victories were nothing short of miraculous, they had also, by their own acts, forfeited all this respect, losing whatever they had gained.

They even did not know that we were a country divided amongst itself, without a strong sense of national unity and with different racial and cultural awareness which they could easily exploit. They treated everyone with the same hostility, disrespect and contempt, uniting all in their dislike of the Japanese nation.

To understand this, it is necessary to give some idea of what was taking place in Malaya at that time.

There was no general consciousness of a Malayan identity at that time. There was not even a Malayan nation. There were nine Unfederated and Federated Malay States at that time under British Advisers and the Straits Settlements consisted of the three colonies of Singapore, Penang and Malacca.

In the case of the Malay states, there never had been a comfortable political situation because the Malays knew that they were being colonised under the guise of protection under the advice of British rulers.

Though the Rulers and their hierarchy were not happy under the British, they were nevertheless comfortable and there were expressions of support for the British as a bulwark against the aggressive Chinese traders that were forever encroaching into the Malay domain with some encouragement from the British who thought they were economically more efficient. This was as much the general expression of the Malay associations formed by the more feudal hierarchy and the senior officer class like Dato Onn Jaafar who was to unite the Malay associations into the United Malays National Organisation (UMNO) to resist the British against the Malayan Union which he considered would destroy the Malay identity and to struggle for independence as a Federation of Malay states.

But hierarchy, obviously feudal and conservative, was opposed in its ideas by a young group of intellectual nationalist Malays which expressed themselves as the Kesatuan Melayu Muda (KMM).

This Kesatuan Melayu Muda was formed in 1938 under the direct influence of Ibrahim Yaacob, Pak Sako and a very young youth leader Boestamam.

Since there was as yet no nation and no Indonesian nation but a number of territories under Dutch and British sovereignty, it was an idealistic idea of young Turks, more anti-colonialists than pro-Japanese elements.

But they were not pro-Chinese either and the Comintern was actively trying to gain their support through a Tan Malaka, working in Indonesia but using Singapore as his watering hole. So, though they were not Communists but Malay nationalists, the British Special Branch had rounded up many of them and had put Pak Sako, Boestamam and some others into Changi prison just before the outbreak of hostilities.

That the Malays were not generally interested in working with the Chinese, whom they viewed as nothing more than businessmen, politically, but wanted to go their own way was also clearly disclosed.

There were a few of the younger and more progressive amongst them who were prepared to work on a non-racial pattern but, though they were nationalists as well they were unable to shift the majority from the umbrellas of Malay organisations.

It is significant to note that though Ishak Haji Mohd and Boestamam were to become leaders in the Socialist Front, the Labour Party and Parti Rakyat, they were never completely happy with the Chinese dominance inside the organisation and that though they tried, they were never able to gain the support of the rural Malays because their parties were not fully under Malay control.

Till the end of their political lives, Pak Sako and Boestamam remained true to their convictions, but remained outcasts amongst most of their own society politically. It is also worthwhile to note that till the end they were both true to their views and when Soekarno launched his odd Confrontation against Malaysia in 1963, it was done under the excuse of the *Melayu* concept.

This idea of Malay dominance was an issue they did not give up until today. It was also how Dato Onn Jaafar was able to unite the Malays.

When Sir Malcolm MacDonald indicated that Britain would only hand over Malaya to a party that had the support of the three major races of the country, the answer by UMNO was to introduce the idea of the Alliance of UMNO, the Malayan Chinese Association (MCA) and the Malayan Indian Congress (MIC) with the UMNO as the predominant party to guarantee that the Malays would not lose their identity and the rejection of Dato Onn's call for a single Malayan organisation.

Onn received a slap in the face and was rejected by UMNO and like the others such as Pak Sako and Boestamam, who were not nationalistic enough, and was, like them, to fade away into the political wilderness had a son who was to become Malaysia's third prime minister as the leader of UMNO.

In 1969, when Tun Dr Ismail, one of the most upright of men whom I had the privilege of crossing swords with many a time in Parliament, returned to service from retirement during the crisis of the May incident of 1969, to assist the Tunku to bring back law and order, the first thing he stressed was UMNO would not give up its position as the party *primus inter pares* amongst its political allies. That was and still is the position today.

That the Malays considered themselves a separate group from the Chinese was known to the Japanese. They were well aware of the situation. From all accounts, the Japanese, who had a network of spies in their photographers and dentists, were very well informed even of the dichotomy between the races and the division between the progressive and the feudal hierarchy.

There were reports that they had even approached some of the young Turks to gain their sympathy and support before the war and one of their very first acts was to set free the Malay nationalists and put British prisoners of war in their place. Yet, they did not seem to take any advantage of this knowledge but chose to treat everyone with the same contempt.

If they could not or did not really try to gain the support of the Malays, they did not fare better with the Chinese either.

Their persecution of Chinese school students in whom they saw the same enemies as the British was drastic to the extreme and if the school students did not care for the British, they cared for the Japanese even less.

The Chinese schools were pro-China and had many pro-China activists, both Nationalist and pro-Communist who were to be found amongst them. Against them, the Japanese could use the same Special Branch and its personnel, even if they were divided between the Kuomintang and the Communists since in both cases they were pro-China and therefore anti-government.

In taking action against them, the Japanese only drove the Left wing into the fringes of the jungle and augment the anti-Japanese resistance forces.

But they also lost the support and respect of another section of the Chinese population, the non-political English-educated. These were Empire and not China orientated. They knew little of Chinese affairs and were therefore not generally dangerous, but they were treated in almost the same way and stood as much risk in a roundup as anyone else.

Traditionally, they were those from whose ranks the government services obtained their recruits. They were people of law and order, not resistance material. But the Japanese lost their support in a peculiar way. These people expect to be treated with dignity and respect. But they were slapped kicked and abused by the Japanese and it went against their grain. Deeply resentful, their emotional response was understandable, they thought the Japanese brutes.

Not only were the people divided racially, but even within the same racial groups and between the English and Chinese-educated. This, the Japanese knew, yet they chose to alienate the feelings of all and sundry, without exception. It was difficult to understand how they could be so disciplined in the battlefield, yet so inept and poor when it comes to winning the hearts and minds of the people.

Strangely, they did not even take advantage of the initial welcome they received from the villages when they first entered the country. They ignored and even turned some of them away. There were reports that they even desecrated their places of worship.

They did make some attempt to form a paramilitary organisation out of some of the more progressive Malay youths but it was soon clear to them that they were treated with some contempt and never seriously.

That Malay support was politically important can be seen from the rumour that when Pak Sako became disillusioned with the Japanese and left the island to return to his home in Pahang towards the end of the war, the news was of sufficient importance that it seemed that a radio signal was sent to Colombo to inform the British that Pak Sako had returned to his home in Pahang from Singapore.

Yet the Japanese did not seem to care. They treated the Malays with so much contempt that they could not muster any mass support for themselves.

The general effect of all this was a negative climate of fear and distrust that the Japanese created for themselves no sooner had they landed. In such an atmosphere, if someone told you he had many friends during the war, you could take it with a pinch of salt. We were on our own and we kept to ourselves. Few but the most foolish exposed their deepest thoughts.

To cap all this, no sooner had they established their rule of terror, they imposed a levy of $50 million on the Chinese population of Penang as war reparations.

To touch anyone's pocket is to hurt him. To touch the pockets of the Chinese without any hope of recompense or public acclaim is to insult him as well. If any millionaire had been eager to welcome them, this was like a cold shower. The millionaires were affronted. They dared not protest because of the risks involved. But it was insult added to injury for their money was in British banks and these banks were closed for the duration of the war.

To bring about a semblance of cooperation, the Japanese appointed Heah Joo Seang, who had traded with Japan before the war and who became known because anti-Japanese elements had invaded his office and set fire to furniture in a protest demonstration. They knew him and appointed him, something that might have seemed more advantageous to him than in reality and they made him responsible for the collection.

To provide him with a greater semblance of dignity and authority, they provided him and his deputy Cheah Seng Kim with civilian uniforms and ceremonial swords.

Cheah Seng Kim was to become head of the MCA in Penang after the war and Heah Joo Seang was to become head of the Straits Chinese British Association which brought him to London with a petition expressing the views of the Straits Chinese for special consideration in the Independence discussions when he was completely ignored.

To show his resilience, when the SCBA failed, he left it and joined the multi-racial Parti Negara, formed by Dato Onn Jaafar after his views were rejected by UMNO, to become a deputy president before it also faded into political oblivion with the failure of the party to gain Malay support.

It was likely that he did not court the post but that it was thrust upon him since the advantage was more apparent than real. His appointment at first caused an unfavourable reaction amongst the people of the island for fear that he was to be the head of a puppet government. But it turned out that all the Japanese wanted was someone through whom they could make demands on the Chinese.

They appointed a Japanese as the Governor of Penang and Eusoffe Abdoolcader became his official interpreter and with that, the civilian government was completed.

The responsibility for collecting fifty million dollars remained with Heah Joo Seang for a war we were never involved in and which we never fought and for which we were not responsible. It was a huge sum, most of the people's money was in British banks and it was not funny to see how many tried to find all sorts of excuses for not coming out with the money and the Japanese not caring how the money was collected so long as it was collected.

The levy was, of course, apportioned, presumably by Heah himself since he was responsible for its payment and he certainly was not about to pay everything himself. Exactly how it had been apportioned no one knew but when my father was asked for his contribution, he flatly refused to pay, maintaining this attitude despite the repeated requests and even when Heah let it be known to him that it was the demand of the Japanese, his invariable excuse being that all his money had been frozen in the British banks.

The real reason for his adamant stand was his shrewd guess that it was irrelevant to the Japanese who would pay and how it was to be collected so long as it was paid. The headache had to be Heah's and he was not about to adopt any of it. He must have been right for he contributed nothing till the end.

But that was how the Japanese brought about the almost universal dislike of themselves, not that people of occupied territories have the propensity to like the enemies of occupation.

Don't sound the trumpets,
Nor trample on those bleeding roses.
War is a tragicomedy that comes
At any time, in any place,
With many masks and faces
And masquerades in many graces.

15. DON'T SOUND THE TRUMPETS

THE fall of Singapore was an act of finality. The people awoke to face a new reality. In the light of continual defeats inflicted upon the Allied forces, it was clear but to the very stubborn, that it would be a long time before peace would come and Japan would be defeated, if at all.

Southeast Asia was not a large single country but a number of small countries which had fallen under the sway of the Western nations with different nationalities. Even Malaysia itself was divided into three Borneo states, nine Malay states and three settlements.

There was some sense of identity in that they were mostly Malay-speaking Muslim sultanates which a group of younger Malays hoped to turn into a Malay-speaking archipelago even if that idea did not have much political support.

There was little sense of a single loyalty and no one had any strong or real role to play in the defence of Malaya. The Chinese-educated, as a group, were probably the only group with a unity of opposition to the Japanese, but only because they considered themselves Chinese who had to resist Japanese aggression in China.

Other than that, the Japanese had a "soft" people to play with, for there was no unity of hostility even if individually, not many liked Japanese aggression.

The English-educated were docile and passively pro-Britain because they were British subjects but luke warm because they were colonial subjects. The Malays were loyal to their separate states which had always resented British suzerainty which they only accepted because they wanted Britain to protect them against the encroachment by the Chinese, There was no such thing as a Malayan race or nationality.

When the people saw how the British collapsed in the face of enemy attacks and, according to the ruthless way Japan dealt with those she thought opposed to her rule, they began to rethink their position towards the war and the Japanese. This was understandable.

The British could not protect them. According to Ian Morrison, some 130,000 British soldiers finally surrendered in Singapore, an appalling number against the small force of 25,000 Japanese pitted against them.

According to Morrison, nearly the same number of civilians (120,000 Chinese civilians) had died in the fighting in Singapore. A Malay officer in a Malay regiment who had fought in the defence of Singapore had been used for bayonet practice in revenge after its fall and some 2,000 local volunteers had been taken to the Changi beaches and slaughtered, leaving a lone survivor who was carried to temporary safety by the tide to tell the tale before he was discovered in a hospital and taken away, never to be seen again.

All this must have had a drastic effect on a people who never knew what war was and who had never been prepared for it. Never again would the Japanese be laughed off as the slit-eyed oriental, the yellow bucktoothed, bowlegged dwarfs of Asia. It was unfortunate for them that they did not live up to the admiration they had gained for themselves through their crude and insensitive cruelty to the people.

Historians always say that history is important because we can learn from it. But that is as far as the body politic is concerned. When the causes of wars are examined as a whole from the national point of view, this may be true. But the national body politic is never the same for the people in charge change and history is not viewed in the same way by different people with different natures and education.

Hitler and the Nazi thinkers did not view the Treaty of Versailles the same way as did its makers and we do not know how much of their argument were excuses for the individual perversions of their leaders for their purpose of starting the march to Germany's greatness. History also attempts to give us different reasons why any war has been started and that there are different reasons for the various wars. But we are not told that often they are for the purpose of gaining territory and for conquests of weaker races. That never quite changes. Every time war is started, it is to redress a wrong and the result is the conquest of part or the entire opposing nation.

The last European war, we are told by some was the result of unfairness of the Treaty of Versailles. But that did not mean that Germany had to conquer the whole of Europe and even beyond. Nor does it mean that Germany had to be united by creating hatred for the Jews.

Even if that is the reason for the war in Europe, it does not explain the Japanese war against the Allies. She had never been oppressed. In fact, she had mostly been the unprovoked aggressor.

And what of the war between Iran and Iraq? They are both Middle East Muslim states, why did they have to go to war? We are told variously that it was engineered by foreign states or that they were struggling for supremacy of the region. Whatever it was, it seemed a war of anger and distrust with righteousness as the emotional background.

Why did Iraq invade tiny Kuwait when they are both dogmatic kingdoms with little democracy? Here we are again given different reasons for it. What of the war in Bosnia-Herzegovina then? Could it be religious if not racial wars?

Surely one can see that war is an armed conflict between states as much as individuals who fight because of religion, race, culture or beliefs because that is the raw nature of man where the highest form of contest is a fight to the death and anger, greed and ego have a great deal to do with it. That, and the belief that one can get away with it.

That, surely, was the reason why Japan's leaders went to war. They went to war because the militarists thought they could get away with it. Had some other leaders with different natures been the leaders, the result could very well have been quite different as post-war Japan has proved it.

The personal element of the leadership has something to do with the type of decision made as different people see things in different light and do not dare the same conclusions as we are all subjective in what we do.

But the tragedy of the innocent caught in the war is always the same, suffering and pain and deprivation and rape are often the result. They are always the victims who have little to do with the war and who would, given the chance, reject the war.

But the innocents were divided people. Though they equally suffered and were in the same position, they were not of the same hearts and minds.

Even as the British defences, hastily thrown up at Slim River after Ipoh, were being just as quickly overrun and as the orders for the withdrawal from Kuala Lumpur were being issued by General Wavell, this division of the people was beginning to be seen, leading to bitter and unwarranted accusations.

The Chinese blamed the Malays for cooperating with the Japanese just because some villages had thought that the Japanese had come to liberate them from the British whom they had never quite accepted.

The police forces returned almost in full strength. To them it was only earning a living. They had no political force or political meaning. To us, they were there merely to keep law and order, whatever the law was so long as the law was the law of the government and the Japanese had become the government.

If the uniformed police returned to barracks, the position seemed to be the same also with the members of the Special Branch. Though they were concerned with "subversives" and "Communist elements" and was therefore political, they did not seem to think so. Though the political structure had changed, they did not think so because there was an overlap between the interests of the British and the Japanese governments. They had nearly the same objectives in the control of subversive elements and the removal of subversives. Therefore, if there was a political element, it did not count. But they returned with a vengeance.

A friend of mine told me that men are born to evil or to goodness. Given the same set of conditions, men would interpret the conditions according to his nature and translate them according to whether he is evil or not. This would echo my belief that wars begin according to the nature of the leaders in power.

Whether we agree to this or not, there is no doubt that war does not encourage restraint. One of its edicts is the destruction of all those who are not in agreement with them and to do away with them "with extreme prejudice", an American term which means to terminate the condition as swiftly as possible.

Given the opportunity, it is strange how evil or brutish some people can become. The Special Branch became an organ of the brutality of the *Kempeitai*. Those put in command by the Japanese, the little men, the lowly, the despicable men, became as feared as the *Kempeitai* itself.

Some of them who joined or rejoined the service saw in their work a chance to work off their frustration, some to work out their viciousness, some with warped mentality cooperated with the enthusiasm of the converted and one of them found himself in the bottom of the sea off Jelutong after the war, a victim of rough justice.

People sought the jobs that suited their nature and, generally, for most of them it was only for security.

The brief delay at Gemas in Johor when only some three Japanese tanks were destroyed or put out of action hardly changed the pace of the war nor did the shooting on the spot of a suspect Chinese who was supposed to have helped direct the Japanese to the position of a field headquarters of the British army helped to change the loyalty of anyone. In fact, though the suspect was supposed to be Chinese, the feeling was that he might have been an infiltrator taken for a Chinese because of his looks which would have accounted for why he could not speak in Malay and refused to cooperate. The Japanese used infiltrators who sometimes dressed in *kampong* or Chinese clothes and he could have been one of them. That he was shot only confused everyone all the more.

Nor did the fighting in Gemas stop the Japanese from reaching the Causeway within four days of the fighting, leading to its surrender on February 11, 1942 in one of the fastest marches to victory ever recorded, having advanced a record of some 500 miles in two months.

Just before the surrender of Singapore, we heard of the formation called the Dell Force under the command of a British officer Dell. It was this force of quickly mustered Chinese-educated volunteers that at first made the Japanese think a Chinese force from China had come to the defence of Singapore. But they were volunteers armed with a shotgun for every six volunteers with six rounds of ammunition each.

It did not do much but it brought about a vengeful Japanese High command who had some of the 2,000 volunteers shot at Changi beaches. If this is not a true story, which I think it is, it makes interesting listening.

There was also a small group of people set up, British style, to carry on the war behind Japanese lines in deep jungle and to carry a new torch of hope and do what the entire British army in Singapore had failed to do.

I think it was at first referred to as the Dell Force but quickly became Force 136. To me they were a bunch of romantics.

They would be traipsing around in the Malayan jungles to gain contact with the Chinese-educated anti-Japanese forces. It was difficult to think how effective it could be since it hardly knew the people or the language or the jungle and when its influence in the towns was almost nil.

From my point of view, Force 136, conceived only as Singapore was about to fall when it was too late to prepare a trained force to work behind the enemy rear, could hardly be effective. It would only cause more embarrassment and provide the Japanese *Kempeitai* with more excuses to wreak havoc on the Chinese living in the jungle fringes than anything else.

If anyone could be effective, it had to be the guerrilla forces and the Dell force could only play a secondary part to it. Anyway, Spencer Chapman has written about them well enough in *The Jungle Is Neutral* for me to pass any more comments.

The end came with the fall of Singapore and any hesitancy to face the situation ended with it. The people began to face the truth as they saw it and began to adjust themselves to the situation as they understood it and it became each man for himself. There was no binding force but that of fear and hatred that was growing.

The author in 1962

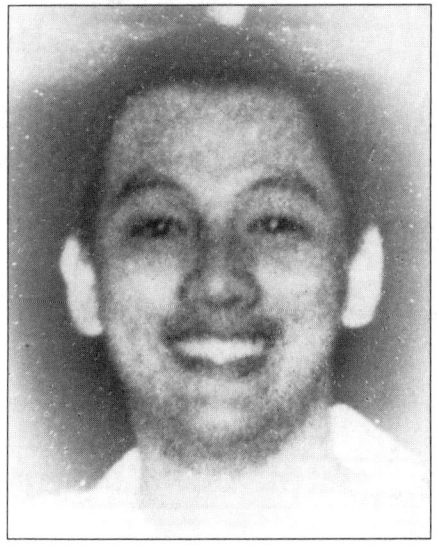

The author in 1942

Back row, standing from left to right: Lim Theng Hin,* Soon Cheng San,* Leong Siew Poh, Yeap Kim Hoe, * S. Kirita San* (civilian officer of Gunseikanbu in charge of the Eposho), Leong ... Kuen,* Koh Sin Hock,* Tan Lip Sun, Khoo Keat Cheong* *Centre row, standing from left to right*: T. Yamagata San (Dy. Officer of Gunseikanbu in charge of the Eposho), Lim Kean Siew, Heah Hock Khoon, Ng Sui Kam,* Khoo Sian Ewe,* Lim Eow Thoon,* Lim Cheng Ean,* Goh Hock Siew,* Dr Ong Chong Keng,* Choong Eng Hye, * Lee Siew Ngock* *Front row, seated from left to right (civilians only; we had not been told who the military officers were)*: Lim Cheng Teik,* Lim Lean Teng* *Note: names with * indicate "since deceased"*

1976: (*from left*) the author and his elder son, Chung Cheng (now Dr Lim Chung Cheng), Kim Hyun Sak, a Korean friend, Suzumu Ogawa and Pamela Ong

At the far end of the picture is the seawall of the Penang Swimming Club in Tanjong Bungah, where the author went for a swim with the Japanese nurses

The Esplanade, Penang, the cast-iron railings were removed by the Japanese during the war and sent to Japan for the manufacture of ammunition and war machines

Crag Hotel, Penang Hill, where Suzumu Ogawa stayed and met the author

Penang Hill Railway, the junction where the Japanese soldiers eased themselves while walking up the hill

The electric tramcars in operation during the Japanese Occupation

An electric tramcar in Penang

A trishaw of the day

Bel Retiro, the governor's resthouse on Penang Hill, a stark symbol of the British Empire

"The Great Wall", a private hill resort built by a wealthy Chinese on Penang Hill

At the top of the hill station which was bombed by the Japanese

A panoramic view of Weld Quay with the Railway Station and Clock Tower in the background

Church Street Pier, built in 1897

*War challenges the norms,
Flaunts the established
Turns loyalties around
And makes heroes out of clowns
Whilst the lowly mock the mighty
And fools dream lofty dreams,
Masquerading with many graces
With many masks and faces.*

16. MANY MASKS AND FACES

THUS the patchwork of life began as people adjusted to the new conditions they found themselves in, interpreting them according to how they understood the facts and making their decisions as they were influenced by their nature and character.

There was the case of an insurance man turned police inspector. His behaviour intrigued for there seemed to be a dual personality in him. He seemed kind and considerate, in fact, sensitive to the feelings of others. But that was not all the time for he seemed vicious and out of character whenever he thought of the power he had as a police officer so much so that he was proud to be known as the "Tiger" of Penang.

He seemed also to take a rather romantic view of his role if he did prevaricate between thinking of himself as an avenger or a minister of justice. Perhaps that was why he was a great admirer of my father who was the civil judge.

"Your father," he used to say, "is a great man, a man of principle and of justice who feared no one. He is the defender of the poor even before the war when he used to save the rickshaw pullers from persecution. I admire men like that, the men who always maintain justice."

But his preoccupation seemed to be with dispensing rough justice in cases where he thought that money had been used against the poor and the needy. But I had a sneaky feeling that this was because of a complex that had developed in him before the war when he had to sell insurance for his living.

It was with delight and a gleam in his eye whenever he reminisced of an opportunity when he had his own back against the rich.

"I like to make the millionaires crawl to me," he said, recalling the occasion, puffing himself up as if with great satisfaction and trying to look larger than life.

"I made him crawl across the room from the door to my desk at the other end of the room. And when he came up to my desk and stood up without my permission, I stood up and went round my desk and without saying a word I gave him a tight slap. Only after slapping him that I asked him who gave him permission to stand up and insisted that he went down on his knees again. Who do you think you are, just because you are rich, do you think you're a big shot?"

He paused, and then added, "Who do they think they are? Big shots?" emphasising his point. One could see that it was the power his commands carried rather than the cruelty he inflicted that gave him more satisfaction.

My friend was an enigma who thought himself to be a Robin Hood of sorts, if he was Walter Mitty as well. He obviously did not do much harm for he was left alone by the British forces in the end.

The war did give opportunities to people like him, some of whom could be seen swaggering around, showing off their authority and waiting for a chance to pounce on anyone they thought they did not like. Most of them, belonged to the *Kempeitai* or those connected with them. They could get away with it because the Japanese had brought fear to the country and terror through the hooded men of the "roundups".

But in the case of the many police officers who were in the police force before the war, there was no enigma. They carried on during the occupation in much the same way as they had done before the war. But without a regular police system and with little accountability to disciplined superior officers, there were of course, more wrongdoings.

It is a fact that those in power tend to abuse their power and where the seniors are also wrongdoers, it is hard to expect their subordinates not to do the same. The top officers who were British, and this statement covered almost all police officers in the rank of inspectors and above before the war but for the new young local inspectors just coming into the force, had all been lost to the force when the Japanese came.

The Japanese did not have trained police officers for our local police force nor were they aware of the many rules and regulations governing the force and so many of the local men were promoted to take on higher jobs for which many of them may not have been qualified either through their training or discipline or education. There seemed to be little regulation discipline and there was a certain laxity which allowed excesses to be taken.

Excesses were committed, especially on the relatives of those who had been arrested when they came to beg for favours and it is not difficult to imagine what this meant, and not all of them had money nor was money always the favour wanted.

Of all of these men there is another character I would like to mention. He was, I believe, a sergeant in the secret society branch before the war and was in his late forties when the war saw him promoted to the rank of inspector, something not unusual, as I have pointed out.

He was old and disciplined enough to know how to behave himself and probably also trained enough to have been an inspector before the war had the policy not to recruit local men not been in force, to let the promotion get to his head. This must be the case for he knew who my mother was and had the greatest respect for her.

So much so that my mother could always go on her bicycle to see him on behalf of the sons of her friends who had been detained by the police. If they were detained in his department they would almost invariably be released a few days later either with warnings or after a few slaps. The relatives did not have to see him but for the occasions when he would send for the mother to tell her what her son had been doing and to hand him over to her care. If they were not detained by his department, he could do little.

In this way, not a few were released and this is not strange for, after the beheading of the two youths, it was common for the people of Penang to leave their doors unbolted. Penang had become crime-free and the secret societies had become inactive.

But though he could exercise his discretion to such a degree, Inspector C did not earn a good reputation for what he did. One cannot say for sure if he was justified, seeing that he was working in the Secret Societies branch. It is difficult to judge anyone in the climate of fear and suspicion and hatred of occupation when everyone was subjectively and emotionally biased.

In any event, one would never know. When the British forces arrived to look for him, Inspector C was nowhere to be found. When I returned from my studies, he was already established in a rather profitable business. It seemed that he had the nimbleness of foot to disappear from Penang to seek refuge elsewhere to evade the storm that was blowing.

Not everyone had such personalities or could hold such high profile jobs. Most took on mundane job with lower profile. But that did not mean that therefore they were less criminal or evil men. Of all, I think, the most distasteful and despicable would be informers and the island seemed to be crawling with them.

Their general excuse, given long after the war when memories had faded and emotions died away, was that they could not find any other job which would enable them not to be sent out of the island. Whilst it is true that an edict, which I will refer to at greater length later, required everyone to take on an accredited job with one of the Japanese organisations, it is questionable if to become an informer is a good excuse.

We were surprised to discover after the war that among them were school friends who had shared with us our meagre rations during the war in our house. They were not only friends but a few of them were close friends. One even became a high-ranking police officer after the war which might indicate that he had done no discovered wrong. His brother, his sister and her boyfriend who was also a frequent visitor to our home were also alleged informers.

This was quite a rude shock and it was fortunate that there was little to report since we had all learnt to keep our opinions to ourselves. They were decent people, young, hale and hearty and hardly out of their teens. They had even come to share our food. My mother would not believe it even if the information was supposed to have come from the British Field Security Services which came in the forefront of the returning army.

There were altogether as many as five or six of them and three of them were so ashamed of themselves that they never again visited our house after they had been exposed. One of them could not even face my brother when he returned. But, in their favour, I must add that we never came to any trouble through them nor do we know of any wrong that they had done.

But there was the case of a beautiful young woman who might have been classified as a sort of *femme fatale* in a more romantic period of history. But neither the situation nor her intelligence qualified her for that role. She was no Mata Hari, she was just unfortunate.

She was arrested by the field security after the war and detained for a few months but was never brought to trial and released without any statement. It was alleged that her beauty was what saved her. But that is only rumour, so no one really knows why she had been detained for so long. One can only feel sorry for her, if that is not being condescending. I wonder if she had been in the United States, she would have sued.

The edict that could have had much influence on their unfortunate decisions was the one that required all men between the ages of fifteen and forty-five, to work within a Japanese organisation or be sent out of the island to the mainland, which was our equivalent of being sent to Siberia.

It must have been issued to push undecided men to cooperate with the Japanese, for it was issued as soon as their government was in place and they were trying to force the previous personnel to return to work, fill the new departments they were establishing and the offices of the Japanese companies that had come to trade.

They tried to involve everyone in their war effort and to make life run once again on the island.

In order to make policing the island easier and to make sure everyone remained indoors during the night, a night curfew was imposed and the island divided into districts each with a head called the *Jikeidancho*. His duty was to set up a roll of volunteers who had to patrol their area to make sure the curfew was maintained. The volunteers he had to choose were those who lived in his area and thus was a record kept of who stayed where. It saved police work and made the island a safer place to sleep in during the night.

The *Jikeidancho* of the city was G.H. Goh, a prominent lawyer. It was fortunate for the *Jikeidan* that the public executions of the two supposed looters were of salutary effect and the city was almost without curfew breakers throughout the occupation for I have no doubt that examples of collective punishment would have been meted out on the *Jikeidans* had there been serious breaches of the curfew.

My father, who seemed impervious to everything was asked to become the civil judge of Penang because of his prominence in the law and because he had been briefly on the bench before the war. He was lucky. His *karma* was good. He did not even have to decide what he should do for the duration of the war. It suited him. It was cut out for him.

When the Japanese finally came to take over from him at Ayer Itam, he was asked to take up the position of a civil court judge to deal with the civil cases pertaining to the locals on civil and land matters and appeals from the lower courts. The Japanese had no interest in such matters and were prepared to let English continue. It offended no political views.

With a serious outlook, a lonely nature, he had always admired the law and its certainty. He had been given something to his liking and in which he was convinced he could do justice. He could bury his head in his law and there need be no heart searching. Principally, he had a judicial temperament, careful not to be over friendly or give any impression that he could be easily approached.

Consequently, the evenings found him either at home or out on his bicycle (he did not even have a car) to see a family, whose members were lifetime friends of his and whose son-in-law was an athlete, a sport he always enjoyed.

All he ever brought home were his basic rations of rice and sugar and pay for the servants. As a result, to survive the war we had to supplement what he could bring home with our own resources.

Lim Khoon Teik returned to his magistracy and two lawyers became the public prosecutors. But the legal establishment was to do with problems concerning local people and affairs. The political crimes remained under the control of the *Kempeitai* and were extrajudicial matters. If anyone was prosecuted after the war it would have been for criminal matters or corruption, civil matters not military ones.

A fellow lawyer of his, Sir Hussein Abdoolcader, also contemporary of my father, chose to occupy himself in an unusual way. If it was not innovative, it was rather funny.

He lived in a house in Pangkor Road not too far from ours but on the way to the Residency occupied by a Japanese Governor. A rather timid, small and inoffensive if rather self-effacing person, one could say what became a habit with him rather suited his personality.

Most of our compound houses have a small drain running across the front just after the side of the road running past the house. Running over this drain there is a small culvert over which the driveway into the compound of the house to the porch of the house, would have to cross. On the sides of this culvert there is a sort of a low parapet to indicate the edge of the culvert. One could sit on this low parapet to enjoy the air or to watch the cars go by.

On this low parapet, it became the habit of Sir Hussein to sit in the evenings just after office hours to enjoy the scene, his neat white shirt and his dark trousers and his small figure, making him look like a penguin, his large hooked nose shifting from side to side as if he was looking for a fish.

Then a strange thing would take place. As one looked and he saw a car with a flag come by, up he would suddenly pop up, and then, facing the car, he would stand, as if at attention and make a ceremonious bow, his hooked nose, oily with sweat from the tropical heat, flashing in the sun, like an off-season penguin without its splendid regalia.

Nor was he really wrong, for those cars with flags carried Japanese personnel of rank and the Governor, and Captain Hidaka at times, would pass and such form of respect could hardly earn points of demerit.

Sir Hussein had a son, a bright student and a linguist with a photographic memory, Eusoffe, who, because of his linguistic ability became the interpreter to the Governor quite early on. He was sent to Japan for further studies by the Japanese and we must presume it was on his own merits that he was sent there.

Eusoffe was in Japan when the war ended from whence he went to London to take his law degree and to end his tragic life as a Supreme Court judge, for he was to commit suicide during his retirement, apparently because of the loneliness after his wife, to whom he was devoted, died.

Sir Hussein continued his practice throughout and was knighted after the war by His Majesty, King George VI, and he died in retirement peacefully.

Japan, I suppose in the best traditions of all colonial powers, tried to impose her culture and thinking and even her understanding of morality on the people. None was spared this determination of establishing the Japanese identity.

All government servants, even those with greying hair, wherever possible, were made to stand to attention and sing the national anthem every morning and do their exercises before returning to their desks. Even schoolchildren when some of the schools were reopened, were made to do the same thing every morning before the start of school.

To us this was strange and it looked like immature attempts at indoctrination. But then, many of the Japanese habits seemed immature and unsophisticated to us.

The unfolding mosaic of war is fascinating. There are so many facets to observe. Some of these were funny, some were tragic. To many of us who had been trained to be tolerant, the suffering was tolerable if sometimes almost unbearable at times. But to accept that one could never tell which of the neighbours were friends or enemies in a war is most trying, especially when there is a desire to know how the war was going.

There was an absolute uncertainty of trust in the atmosphere; fear and suspicion stalked the land and moved into every home by stealth to push out the faith and security one had come to expect in every home. New habits of hypocrisy, slyness and cunning quickly overtook that of openness and trust. One became uncommunicative, kept two faces, one for the public and the other when one faced oneself in the middle of the night.

One even began to question the meaning of God. Yes, strangely, in such moments when the meaning of morality is important to decide how one should behave, it is fear and survival that decide.

My mother believed that marriages are not made in heaven but are the result of the interplay of human nature. This, I had come to believe, was also the truth about wars. All reasons are in fact excuses to bolster the war we inflict on others.

It is the human nature as well as the karmic forces. To me, the world is like us individuals, it is also an organisation in which we are like a corpuscle as it is also a corpuscle in our galactic universe which is also only a larger organism that lives and generates itself and keeps itself in balance to one day also die away.

Like all organisms and organisations, it is also the result of its own causes and results as it moves along and adjusts itself to changes of its surroundings. That is a scientific view for science believes there is no cause without an effect and no effect without a cause. The cause causing the effect which then becomes the cause itself in turn.

That being so, how much blame can we apportion to each individual caught in this mad world of war when they are only reacting to causes as they feel it? Was not every one of us only reacting according to the dictates of our nature which has also affected the way we think and believe?

So with the individuals, so with the nations and their rise and fall. Thus, China had been great, then India, the Middle East, Greece, Italy, Spain, Portugal, Holland, Britain, the United States, and now the circle was completing and it was the time once again of the Far East led by Japan and who knows if it will be China again?

This is also the argument of the Chinese geomancy and the Taoist schools with their mysterious calculations, which, for all their mystery, is based upon the planets and the stars and the cycle of the nine planets which falls into a straight line once every sixty years.

The beginning of the fall of the old Empires had come and Japan was having her day and so were the individuals who were waxing firm. But her time was not yet. She would be suffering from the Bomb and she would have to atone for her wrongs.

But she was to open our eyes. Before the war everything was simple. We had a placid life and everything was accepted without question. The world seemed stable enough and Britain could demand loyalty which was generally given without challenge.

We saw the certainty of law, of the superiority of the West, of the stability of Britain and the Empire. Japan was changing all that.

But many things were changing too. Loyalty now meant loyalty to Japan and therefore we began to ask its meaning. Morality meant Japanese *Kempeitai* morality so its meaning also came under challenge. Honour and sacrifice now meant honour and sacrifice in the name of the Emperor and this put on its head the argument that there can only be one loyalty or that honour and sacrifice could never be reread according to who is in power since honour to one can be treachery to the other.

You can imagine how difficult it became. For example. Ian Morrison, in his book on the Malayan campaign referred to the killing of someone suspected of having acted against British interests. To those who shot him, that man was treacherous. But then, he might have been a Taiwanese and to the Japanese he might have been a hero of the war.

For the first time in our life, we could see the British were just as foreign as the Japanese. For the first time, many began to question the meaning of being a subject race, for few, if any, wished to be a subject of a Japanese Empire.

Even the meaning of god was threatened. Who is God when everyone is talking of victory because their gods supported their cause. My mother's view, though she sent us to Sunday school, was that everything was the result of *karma*, begs the question. *Karma* to her is something of fate, something in us that has decided what would happen to us. It looks backwards and then professes a truth after the event. But it is an interesting view for it does not require analysis but only understanding—a man is what he is because that had been decided by his *karma*.

All these points of view become important if we have to judge the acts of everyone during the occupation. For example, would a colonial subject be a quisling if he worked for the Japanese? Would he be a hero if he worked for the British? Would that not depend on who is making the judgement?

I finally gave up speculating. In the reality of life it is difficult to decide what should be the precedent. Judgement becomes difficult. Problems have too many facets. Fear and the need to survive place on morality a materialistic character. Furthermore, it is difficult to know what and how people think for most of us have learnt to put on two faces, one for the world to see and the other for our world within, to shield us from the world.

*War can be a tragicomedy
And whilst the actors strut about,
Play little masquerades with masks
To mock the brooding adversity,
The slaughter marches on behind
The clownish gestures and graces.*

17. A TRAGICOMEDY

TO know how difficult it is to judge anyone, let me tell you of an incident where those involved were not strangers but teachers who knew one another and me and even my family, yet behaved as if they were enemies and not friends from the same overrun country.

Why they should have done what they did was something inexplicable for they acted, not on the ground that we should all help protect ourselves in times of adversity but with the animosity of the converted.

Woo Lin Heng had been one of my teachers at the Francis Light Primary School. He had become unemployed during the Occupation because he had refused to work for the Japanese, choosing to hawk local cakes produced by his wife.

"Cakes," he replied. "Would you like some?"

He approached us and lifted the cover of his carrier. What I saw was pitiful. Even if we bought the entire basket, I knew it would hardly suffice for his upkeep.

Even the way he looked was sufficient to tell and he did not have to tell me that things were hard for him. The cakes were made by his wife and he had thought that would be sufficient. But it was not. He would not be able to earn enough for the family to survive for long. I did not ask him why he had not taken a job. Obviously he could have as other teachers had done. But he had chosen to be loyal to his beliefs that working for the Japanese was not right.

Instead, I asked if he could let us each have a cake. They were actually curry puffs but in his anxiety to sell something, he had merely said what sounded most pleasant to his ears.

How long had he been selling cakes? I asked. Did he have many customers? The way he looked in answer was sufficient. He did not have to answer me.

Would he like a job? I asked, for if he would not take a job with the Japanese, I was sure he would not refuse me if he wanted one and I could see he was desperately in need of a job. A schoolteacher is usually not a very practical person when it comes to such things.

It was a rather humiliating situation for him to have to be offered a job by a former student and not being in a position to turn it down. To make matters easier for him, I changed the subject and bought his entire basket for my staff and proceeded to pay him for it.

Taking the payment and counting the change helped him to hide some of the sudden flush that had come to his face. It was relief and he was near to tears. Recovering as he handed me the change, he explained that his wife was not really cut out to be a cook neither was he a suitable person as a hawker. He and his wife were only trying to earn an honest living.

To save him any further embarrassment, I told him the pay was not good, I think I mentioned the figure of two hundred and fifty dollars a month but I added, "I need someone to help me. It's only a sundry shop and I hope you do not think the job too small for you. But there were always leftovers of rice and sugar to which the staff is entitled. At least in that way we can save ourselves from starvation!" Then we both laughed and the embarrassment was gone.

He was born with a slight deformity. His mouth did not sit straight on his face. It was twisted to one side as if in permanent sarcasm and it twitched. Sitting on a face emaciated by miles of daily walking and insufficient food, its malformation had become more obvious.

He looked at me. Quizzically, I thought, with his mouth twisted to one side. Then he whispered a quiet "thank you", and added, "Can I start work tomorrow? I would like to go home and tell my wife the good news first."

The gratitude and the relief he showed was sufficient recompense.

That was how Woo Lin Heng came to work for his former pupil. It was a spontaneous little offer on my part but it was to save me from a possible incarceration by the *Kempeitai* later on. But I was not to know that then.

For it was Woo who saved me from the two former schoolteachers who had chosen to work in the Food Control Office, the office that did the work the name suggests. One of its duties was to keep a check on the passage of controlled items, which meant all food that was not rationed. It was not much of a job, only that it issued permits for the transmission of goods from shop to shop to prevent them from falling into the hands of the terrorists which had the same meaning to them as it did to the Japanese.

It was these two who had once come to check on my stocks and when they found there was some shortage had threatened me with the *Kempeitai*.

Perhaps they were born to do mischief as Woo was born to do goodness. Maybe he was one whose moral compass had kept steady in the turmoil of war. He was over forty-five and he had not joined his colleagues and he had betrayed no one. He had chosen his life without misgivings or heart searching as my father had done except that he had not been so lucky. But equally he had not fawned nor bowed nor given way.

He was later to save me from possible incarceration in a Japanese prison in this way.

Towards the end of the war, someone, for some strange reason, must have betrayed me. It must have been someone very close and who knew my business methods.

As a wholesaler, I sold in retail to sundry shopkeepers all through the island. It was their practice to place their orders in the morning. Delivery would take place in the afternoons when they would come with their transports on their way home. The goods were food items such as maize tapioca flour, molasses and so on, all subject to food control permits supposedly to prevent them from going into the hands of the "subversives" in the jungle though the island hardly had any really active "subversives".

Permits could only be applied for after we had sold our goods in the morning and delivery and payment had to be made in the afternoons. But though the permits were applied for and approval obtained, they were not issued until the next morning. It was important that we had to allow for delivery in the afternoon because we wholesalers had to pay for our goods in cash even though we could delay payment till the evening when the accounts were closed for the day by disappearing from our shops till after bank closing time. Thereafter, we could even pay by account payee cheque which meant that the cheque would not be cleared till the afternoon the following day when the banks also closed their accounts.

One afternoon, probably based on information received, those two schoolteachers I have mentioned who were known to me and my family, paid a surprise visit to my wholesalers' premises and discovered the shortage which were goods for which permits had been submitted but not yet issued and which I had allowed delivery.

It was not a serious offence as the permits had been approved. It was only that the stamping of such approvals mostly took place the morning after since the officer would often leave work early. But something in their manner told me they were there looking for trouble. It was not a routine check because they seemed to know what they were looking for.

I tried to convince them that permits had been applied for and approved and their delay was only in the stamping of the approval. I even suggested that as we were all locals and they could overlook this as it was a technical matter. I pointed out to them that if I had waited for the permits I would have lost the sales and not be able to meet payment of cheque issued. It was to no avail.

Finally, I threw my last card in. All these foodstuffs were for us, the locals, not the Japanese and surely they could simply go home and return the next morning and the matter would automatically have been sorted out by then.

They were completely unmoved. I began to wonder if they knew who their friends and enemies were any longer. I hinted that the Japanese government was a hostile government and there was no need to go so far in the execution of their duties.

But they were equally adamant that I had breached the regulations. Asking me to sign their findings in their books and that I would be reported to the *Kempeitai* the next morning, they left the shop.

Woo, meanwhile, further up the road in my sundry shop, had heard of their raid. As soon as they left the shop, he came and we had a brief discussion. It was time he repaid my kindness, he said. Then, after a brief thought, he came up with a proposal.

"Never mind," he said, "I know them. They only live a few doors away from me in the same school quarters. Give me two bags of ten *gantangs* of rice each and two bags of fifteen katies of sugar each and I will see what I can do."

I instructed our staff to fulfil his request and he soon went off to their homes and we waited patiently and anxiously.

Shortly after eight that evening he returned, beaming. He had done his job. The rice and the sugar had been received with gratefulness. I was to go and collect the permits as usual the next morning and they would come and check the store again. They came in due course and, as they were leaving, they found that I had changed the name of the shop. Perhaps they had thought to close my business down as they had every right to do. But I had also prepared for such eventualities. To prepare for such unforeseen emergencies, I had taken the trouble to register, under the same premises, several businesses so that if one was closed down I could open another one immediately. In anticipation of their closing down my business, I took out a license from this stack and proceeded to carry on my business under the new name.

I had not intended them to know this but as they were leaving a customer came to give instructions as to when we should prepare to deliver him the goods he had already purchased that morning. He did not know what was happening or who the two gentlemen (who were about to leave the shop) were.

There was a rubber stamp with the name of the new business and the receipt produced by the man to show us what we were to prepare for delivery to him, the cat was out of the bag. Fortunately, they could not do much in view of what had taken place the night before.

They could but make a show. How come I was trading under the name of Kean Guan instead of Kean Swee Trading under which I had been trading. I explained that I had two licenses. They then asked why I had not taken down the old signboard. They had not cancelled my license and it was doubtful if they would. I had only decided on this course of action as a precautionary measure and in anticipation.

Frustrated, they insisted that I take it down. I simply explained that I could not do that till all my debts were collected and my goods paid for, explaining that if I took down my signboard it might be mistakenly thought that I had closed down the business. After all, I added, one does not take down one's father's picture simply because he had passed away.

As soon as they stormed out of the building, I fell to wondering who was right or wrong. I even wondered if we should not, in the final analysis, judge people on the grounds of common decency. But then, what does common decency mean to each of us.

When I told my mother of the incident, she just shrugged it off. What will be will be. After all, I did not get into trouble and they didn't get enough for their needs to make much difference. That was how

Penang went through the occupation, each adjusting to the conflicts and surviving, each living in his separate world with different moral justifications and it was really the war that Japan brought that was the cause.

"In all the four seas, all men are brothers."

How strange.

Even as the world shuts its eyes in shame
To see rivers run with blood and
The very earth stained a scarlet red,
Some still search the wind and the sky
To see if the world still sings.

And, in the middle of the night,
We try to turn nightmares into sweet dreams
As we wait in hope to see the sun
Nudge the dark night and dawn's banners
Slap to life fading hope itself.

18. THE WORLD SHUTS ITS EYES

SO, whatever we believed in, we had to do what we could to survive, even in a sick way as life had to go on. I had made my decision early but it was more instinctive than reasoned.

In striking out on my own independently, I was encouraged by my mother who believed that no matter what I chose to do, I would meet with hostility but, like the doll that would never topple over, I would survive. I liked that, after all my decision was to trade in essential foodstuffs and that automatically meant survival.

Since the Japanese government tried to control everything, it meant working outside of the Japanese government environment. It meant working within the Chinese-educated environment, in the fringes, shaving the law, it meant not doing what was "right and proper".

But I was easy. As I have said, it was each man to his own judgement and I did not consider the Japanese government legitimate and there was no reason why I should carry on as if everything was normal when it was an Occupation.

To understand the situation, rationing did not mean any assurance that the government would give us enough to live on, even if we could survive on it. We had to supplement our food with our own resources outside of the rationed food, eating such as *ragi*, or millet, and dried tapioca chips and yam if we could get them.

But the Japanese government did not leave me alone to carry out my plans. Even as I was preparing to establish my firm of importers, exporters and wholesalers, which was to allow me the possibility of travel to and bring in from Kedah and Thailand those necessary foods.

The edict requiring everyone between the ages of fifteen and forty-five to register for evacuation out of the island to work in the agricultural sector or their railway to the north of the island in Burma unless we could show we were working with one of the arms of the military, the government or in one of the Japanese organisations.

It was a blow, for I was not even registered in the *Jikeidan* and it was full. When I saw the edict, my heart sank. But it was to be a blessing in disguise.

There were fifteen categories of employment listed there beginning with employment in the *Kempeitai* and the police. This was not what I wanted. On the other hand, being sent to Butterworth for agricultural work was equally bad. I was no labourer and agricultural work in Butterworth meant working in leech and malaria-infested padi fields to which we were not accustomed and to be hit by the malaria fever meant inevitable suffering for the illness can be a recurrent one. It was like being sent to Siberia.

But the sixteenth item on that list held promise. "Mechanic" brought about exemption and there were no exams to pass. Anyone who could work on a car was a mechanic of some level or other. If someone could register me in his workshop as a mechanic I was safe.

But I was no mechanic. All I knew about engines was how to tune my motorcycle and how to strip it down for decarbonising the cylinder head. Who would want a novice?

But I saw a glimmer of hope as the family of a motor garage which sold cars were family friends and we were one of their valued customers since all our cars were purchased through them. Besides, the wife had played tennis on our court.

The garage was about half a mile from where I was operating and so it was convenient for me since I never really had any intention of being a full time mechanic. All I wanted was an address and part-time work. I approached the brother-in-law of the owner. He stalled for a night and told me the next morning that the boss could not agree with my proposal in case the Japanese should come and discover the cover up. The risk of getting into trouble with the *Kempeitai* was too great.

Having failed to convince him to change his mind, I had to find an alternative quickly. By then, I had learnt enough from the Chinese business community not to feel sorry for myself.

If necessity is the mother of invention, desperation is the father of innovation. I quickly formulated another plan which was to prove useful even if it brought risk a few times.

If no one would employ me, could I not employ myself? No qualification was required for anyone to open a garage. Why should I not open one? The answer stood up in my face clearly. I would set up a garage and a workshop myself.

It would not be difficult to find someone also looking for a job who could come in with me as a mechanic if I could set up a garage.

I had a school friend who was from a family of mechanics whose father was a motorbike specialist. Seng Hock could repair bikes. He had repaired my bike and Lim Seng Chye had helped on occasions and I knew he was a mechanical genius who became a top mechanic in Fiat's without having to go through an engineering school.

We were all from the same school and we were all in the same boat and looking around to escape the dragnet.

I made my proposal to them. We would find premises to set up a garage and I would finance it provided that they joined me and I would be taught as quickly as I could learn. That way, we could all register as mechanics and work instead of just hanging around. Of course, I was not hanging around but I could not exclude myself in our discussion.

In no time at all, we had found an old empty building with a huge piece of land on which attap sheds for a workshop and garages could be put up quickly. It had been used as a Chinese kindergarten and primary school before the war and no way would it be allowed to start up again. The rest of our plans fell into place.

The Japanese army had taken away all usable trucks and lorries. There was a shortage of transport. Just before the war, old Ford trucks had been taken off the roads and their places had been taken up by new trucks with more cylinder engines.

In the junk shops lay these old Fords stripped down for spare parts. If they could be reassembled they could be used as civilian transports and they would be safe from the Japanese since they would be too old for military use.

For fuel, we would set up small burners on our lorries, using scrap rubber as fuel. The burners would boil the scrap rubber, which was considered waste material, and the fumes would take the place of petrol for the engines. It was an idea thought out by the Chinese transport engineers as a way of circumventing the fuel shortage brought about by the war.

Building a vehicle from scratch with parts from the scrap heap may not be everybody's idea of learning mechanical skills but it was to me; and building an entire vehicle this way was the fastest way to learn. Soon enough, I had become a sort of mechanic, if not a good one. By the time the few old Ford truck frames had become completely built up lorries, I had become a competent mechanic.

The Japanese had also confiscated all new tyres they could find. For tyres, we had to make do with retreads. To retread tyres, I set up a retreading workshop at the back of my retailers. It did not require much space for all that was required was a charcoal burner with clamps to which an old tyre for remolding could be clamped with its raw retread to be cooked over the charcoal fire. The mould would remould a quarter of a tyre at each cooking and the remould was good enough at a time when there was a shortage of tyres even if they had a tendency to peel whilst in use at high speeds.

It was a slow and time consuming process but it worked and such a small workshop was easily set up. So, using the rear portion of local products I became a tyre retreader in tandem with our "assembly" plant.

All this was a new exhilarating experience for us even if it was to provide some rather bizarre incidents. Then, just as we settled down two young naval officers from the 2944 Butai, the naval group running the naval base in Penang, came to the garage and told us they wanted to "adopt" our workshop for the Navy. "Adopt" is a vague term. But there could be no objection. Fearing the worst, we asked them what they meant.

The Navy required workshops, they explained. They had come to us in case the Army came first. In the final analysis, we were the only workshop they "adopted" and it was never clear to us why this was the case.

We could only surmise that there was fear that the Navy might be subject to air raids from the British Far East naval base set up at Trincomalee in Ceylon by Mountbatten, which, in the event, never materialised.

It was this that turned out to be a blessing in disguise because they put up a "2944 Butai" signboard on one of the pillars of the gates and gave us a pair of number plates with a navy anchor sign and we were left in peace by the Army.

In fact, even the navy never came except on one Friday morning when two Japanese naval civilians turned up with a Rover car bearing a navy number plate. They were on their way to Bangkok but their car was giving some trouble which they wanted us to fix up.

We gave the car a quick once over. There was a whine from the rear which could only come from a worn crown and pinion gear in the back axle. There was not even the need to open the gearbox to confirm this. It was usable but the proper thing to do was to change the crown and pinion if spares were available.

A Rover was the car used by majors in the British army and British planters in our rubber estates. If there were any spare parts to be found, it had to be in Ipoh as it was a rare model in Penang. That led me to think of using the car for an Ipoh weekend as I had a friend who had married in Penang and who was anxious to return home to Ipoh to visit his parents. I, too, had a friend I wanted to see there.

Travel away from home was then a rare adventure few felt safe enough to attempt. This was a heaven sent opportunity too rare to miss. The car was a naval car; it had a navy number plate which meant that it only came under navy control and I was confident no sentry would stop us on the public road all of which meant permission to travel out of the island with some assurance of safety.

The owners of the car were travelling on to Bangkok and wanted to have the car fixed up properly before they undertook the journey.

I told them I would have to go to Ipoh to find those parts and asked them to return the following Monday.

I had to tell them I would have to look for parts in Ipoh because I intended to use their car for the journey. I did not actually tell them my intention in so many words but sufficiently to allow me the excuse, should anything happen to us on the road, to say that I had in fact asked for permission to use their car.

Nor did I tell them the rest of my intentions which were to use the car to take my friends down to Ipoh and to see my friend. The next morning found me on my way to Ipoh with the friend and his two female relatives, with Seng Hock in tow.

It turned out to be quite an escapade. We arrived safely, with no undue excitement. There were no sentries on the road.

Having installed my friends with their relatives, I looked for my friend. The next morning, Henry Putra and his brother, both motoring enthusiasts, took Seng Hock and I to a coconut plantation to have some toddy, a wine of coconut sap fermented on the tree with yeast.

I must say that this was at my request because I wanted to know what toddy fresh from the tree tasted like. I did not know what it was but soon after the arrival of the Japanese, when toddy was withdrawn from public sale, the Indian developed beri-beri due to a shortage of vitamin B in their diet. This, it was said, came from toddy which was extracted from the sap dripping from the main stump of a clump of young coconuts which had been sliced off.

The sap is gathered in a pot attached to the stump into which a bit of yeast had been introduced which allowed the sap to ferment even as it was gathered.

It is a nice tasting alcoholic liquid and we sat down beneath a coconut tree to enjoy its delicious taste. What happened next was not at my request.

My mischievous friend sat us down beneath a tree and supplied us with a few dishes of strings of rice vermicelli called *kutumayom* wrapped up in banana leaves. He had told us he would supply us with breakfast and this was his breakfast.

Kutomayom is normally taken with sugar and freshly grated coconut. Being rice vermicelli and therefore can be fermented in yeast. Sugar is also a carbohydrate and in liquid form it can accelerate the process of fermentation. In the presence of toddy, it becomes a highly potent substance.

They did not tell me all this. He and his brother were waiting in anticipation to see what would happen to me, knowing full well that I was returning to Penang that afternoon.

By mid-morning, I was completely drunk. But it was not the worst. By early that afternoon, I was having the worst hangover I had ever had as the rice continued to ferment within me. Their devilment had paid off; they had the satisfaction of seeing their friend drunk in the midst of an estate in Ipoh which was a centre of anti-Japanese activities.

Late that afternoon, I began my drive back to Penang. I had never questioned the definition of friendship, nor was I cautious with friends in the presence of alcohol. The lesson I learnt was put to good use later in politics for I never again was to be caught offguard or drunk.

The journey back took some three hours by road at that time. We left at four, planning to reach home just before sunset. I was too drunk to leave before then and it would be nearing curfew time. It was already late but all would be well if nothing untoward happened on the journey home and I would be ready for the owners of the car who were coming for it on Monday morning.

We had just passed Nibong Tebal, about twenty-one miles from the island, when the rear left wheel and shaft of the car rolled off the car and ended in an irrigation drain on the side of the road. We never expected this to happen. In fact, such incidents rarely happened under normal conditions.

Dusk was already gathering and it was a Sunday. It was the bearing of the shaft that held the axle to the shaft housing that had broken loose. There was nothing to do but to look for a replacement.

Leaving the rest in the car, they behaved pretty well under the circumstances, Seng Hock and I took out the remnants of the bearing for its size and trudged back to the small village. But all the shops were already shut. We knocked on the door of a small foundry, it was the best place to find a replacement. Someone answered from inside the house but no one came to open the door.

There was only one foundry but we tried a few doors to see if anyone was prepared to take us in for the night as we did not want to be caught out in the open. In fact, no one opened any doors that evening.

That was a misfortune. There was nothing we could do. We were in a strange town. To the householders we were strangers whom they had no reason to trust. We got no accommodation and we had to return to the car with the sad news. There was no other choice but to sleep out in the car in the open.

We were on the main and the only North South highway. There was every risk that we would be spotted by Japanese troops if they should choose to move in the night. Anyone on a journey along that road would not miss the car and its occupants.

As the darkness gathered, swarms of mosquitoes began to keep us company. It was not a comfortable night. We could hardly sleep. But that was more of a nuisance than a worry.

Then, in the still of midnight, there came through the impenetrable darkness, the ominous sounds of what sounded like a squad of soldiers on the march down the road. As the sounds came nearer, we even heard sounds of breathing and what sounded like the striking of heavy boots on the metal of the road.

"Soldiers," someone quietly whispered the dreaded word into the hush of the car. There was an imperceptible catching of breath as everyone prepared for the worst.

I thought quickly. The steps came from the north. If the girls quietly left the car and went as far forward up the road as they could before the soldiers arrived and then went into the canals and kept quiet, it was possible that the soldiers would come upon the car to find the men there sleeping in it for it was what I decided Seng Hock and I should do.

They would then assume that we were the only two and take whatever action they wanted with us. But with three wheels on the car, even they would understand the situation. But should they be suspicious and decide to look if there were others, they would look around the area and a bit beyond it down the road. It was not so likely that they would look back in the direction from which they came as those who are afraid would tend to move away from the source of danger and therefore to the south and behind the car instead of in front of it.

As quietly as I could, I opened the door for them and the women began to creep forward up the side of the road as fast as they could go with my last instructions tingling in their ears that they were to make themselves as invisible as possible by going down the side of the monsoon drain and staying below the level of the road and, should anything happen to us, they were to ignore it and get into the plantation beyond the canal and stay there till the soldiers had departed from the scene.

Seng Hock and I then prepared ourselves to sleep in the car and be ready with our explanation that we were working for the Navy (in view of our number plate) and that our car had broken down and we were waiting for the dawn to have it repaired. In the event, no explanation was necessary.

As the footsteps came nearer and as I could discern dim black shapes marching, seemingly in ranks, I suddenly heard the voice of an Indian shouting and cracking a whip.

Relief flooded through me when the looming shadows suddenly materialised themselves into a herd of water buffaloes being driven down the road by their keeper.

The shouting of the keeper was because of his sudden fear when he had suddenly been taken aback as he saw the unmoving object on the road in front of him which was our car just at the same time as when we were able to discover that the shapes in front of us were his water buffaloes.

It was mutual fear and after the initial shout to give himself some Dutch courage, he fell into silence as he drove his herd past the car without even sparing a moment to find out if it was empty.

Seng Hock began to laugh with relief. I called out to the ladies to come back to the car and, in a few moments, they returned, still creeping and in silence. After a while, we again settled into a restless sleep.

As dawn touched our eyes with its half light, we stirred and began to work out the problem. There is no way any bearing can be repaired. We had to find a substitute. We decided to go back to the small foundry whilst the rest followed to look for a wash and a bite. We looked for a bearing and found one but it was not a Rover bearing. It was for a Morris. Not only was it too narrow and had to be broadened to fit the housing and the inner core too large for the shaft. But the outer diameter fitted the housing and so our problem was reduced to two.

To fit the bearing to the shaft, two small pieces from an old clock spring were inserted to take up the slack between the bearing and shaft and driven home to make certain that the shaft would not run loose. Whether it would work could only be known in actual use when the car was running on the road since it had never been done before. Spring steel was the hardest steel I knew at that time and it was the best I could think of. I was hoping that part of the bearing being friction being as it was the unmoving part of the bearing, the idea would work.

But the bearing was also too thin to sit in the housing properly. To cure that we looked for a piece of water pipe which could fit the housing. We then cut off a piece of sufficient width to make up for the thinness of the bearing and laid the bearing against it in the housing and locked the bearing into place.

That was all we could do under the circumstances of the war. The water pipe was a thin one and it was not strong, nor did it have sufficient depth. But it took up the sideways slack; the small pieces of steel spring held the bearing tightly against the shaft.

It was not perfect but it was the best we could do. It could work. Whether it would work when the car started to run on the road remained to be seen.

Hoping for the best, though with some trepidation, I slipped the car off the chocks, started the engine and shifted it into gear and gingerly stepped on the accelerator.

The car moved forward. It seemed to work. Soon, we began to increase our speed and then held the car at a reasonable cruising speed. Everything held and by the time we reached the ferry to go across the channel we were already driving at a normal speed.

We reached home before the offices opened. Not only had we failed to find any spares but it now had also lost an original bearing to its rear shaft and there was no telling how long our repairs would take.

To correct the gearbox whine, we packed the gearbox up with saw dust to thicken the gearbox oil. It would do for a while.

When the owners turned up for the car that Monday at noon, a cleaned and polished car was waiting for them. They were going to Bangkok and the car had been supplied to them for that purpose. They did not know about the condition of the car. So long as they reached Bangkok on schedule, they would be happy.

Till then, the Japanese face was a face in an amorphous front of war. We distinguished no individual face we could separate from that amorphous bunch; it was only a face of the enemy that we saw and the impression was that as depicted by propaganda and fear.

For the first time, what I had dimly discerned when the naval officers had come to "adopt" our garage, I saw the human individual face behind that war front.

They were very polite. They bowed to us whenever they could. They paid close attention to what we were saying. They were doing their duty. They were under instructions to get to Bangkok within that week and they had to make it. I did not think they were so much concerned with the war as with carrying out instructions. I found that they were disciplined, that they were schooled and involved. In a way that the disciplined schoolboy is different from the street urchin who had never known the discipline of school.

There was a reciprocal feeling we could feel rising in us when they began to explain their difficulties and their lack of suspicion. Seng Chye, who was with me, felt the same thing he told me later when we discussed the matter after they had left.

He interjected at that point and began to explain to them that what they had was a car that had probably been used on rough dirt track estate roads which could explain the gearbox whine. It was also probable that other parts had been weakened which would tell on their journey to Bangkok. That would explain the repairs we had done on the rear shaft but would not necessarily implicate us.

The older of the two explained that they had to take what was given and it was their duty to get on to Bangkok. He apologised for causing us so much trouble and insisted on paying us.

I cannot remember if they did eventually pay us. We had not expected any payment. We were relieved that it was only repairs that they had come for. The relief was more valuable than any payment. Whether the car served them well till they reached their destination in Bangkok we never knew. They never came back. Nor did we hear anything more from them.

It was a pleasant interlude. We had an escapade and we had got away with it. It was a relief from the eternal gloom of the war. We had, in other words, got away with it and, having done so, we could now see that there was also some humanity and human failings on the other side.

For even in the gloomiest times,
Flames still burn in kindred souls
That can spark and rekindle
The humanity within our hearts
As do earth's eternal fires
Bring back from beneath cold winter's
Crust of ice, the rites of spring
And the warmth of summer which even
Cold late frosts of winter cannot kill.

19. WINTER CANNOT KILL

THE chink through which we had found some humanity behind the cold front of the war, even if the human relief came in the form of the two naval men, opened a bit further when I met two Japanese nurses on leave in Penang during what appeared to be the darkest hours of war, after wave upon wave of Japanese victories at sea pitched their forward lines so close to Australia that they were virtually staring down at the sea coasts of northern Australia.

Teong Kooi was a school friend some three years older than I. Since I was fourteen when I met him and he was seventeen, he was a strong youth whilst I was little more than a puny little boy and that made a lot of difference so much so that I had come to look to him as an elder brother. Moreover, he was a strong youth, a state water polo player and a school swimmer, he was the very companion I would look for whenever I went for a swim in the sea. At the beginning of the war, I thought to go swimming and who but Teong Kooi could I bring along as a companion.

So it was that we found ourselves swimming in the Penang Swimming Club where we met these two young nurses. We had, at first, taken to swimming in the sea off the Chinese Swimming Club which at that time had no swimming pool.

The sea was the only thing that seemed bigger than the Japanese and unmoved by the holocaust of war. Swimming in the open sea alone was embalming and gave us a sense of freedom, an escape from the oppression of war. But the seas of Penang were seldom free of jellyfish and it was not long before we decided to look for safer areas to swim in. Soon we began to be stung.

So, one day, venturing a little way up the coast we noticed that the Penang Swimming Club, the exclusive haunt of the British, had fallen into disuse. A closer look revealed that the pool was empty though the club was still immaculately kept and the pool was sparkling clean.

There was a caretaker present who still took his job seriously. Indeed, there was a coffeeshop in the club. The club itself, though deserted, seemed also dust free. He was more than happy to see us. No one used the swimming pool any more, he lamented. The Japanese did not swim and the locals were afraid of venturing out of doors. We were certainly welcome to use both the pool and the coffee facilities in the club itself.

We took a quick look round the club. Everything seemed the same. The building and the pool, built practically on a rock face dropping sharply into the small bay beyond, were set on solid foundations and would last for many more years. The building itself was a mix of concrete foundations and solid hardwood which was obviously meant to withstand the sea water and spray.

Behind the open verandah, with its low railings stretching the entire front of the main building, seemingly to reach over the thin shore line below and which provided a beautiful view of the Penang channel and Kedah peak beyond, the islands standing in between, and the site of the early Sri Vijaya Indian settlement below which had existed over a millennium ago, stood the long bar over which drinkers would drool, now forlorn and empty. To the right along the shoreline as one stood facing the sea, was the huge swimming pool with sparkling clean water and without the smell of human bodies and the imposition of the human ego.

Like all colonial structures, the club breathed a sedate, quiet and confident atmosphere as if to keep good the claim that the sun would never set over it as a symbol of the British Empire. Even now, empty, there was that serene air about it which reminded me of this boast. It was inviting enough to tempt us to overcome all hesitancy and prejudice.

It was not long before we were sufficiently assured to change into the costumes we had brought with us.

For the first few weeks, nothing eventful disturbed our routine. No one came to the club, we swam alone and in complete freedom and in complete peace as if the pool had been built for us.

Then, on a Saturday, the chink on the iron face of the war, opened by the two Japanese naval men with their Rover, opened further to display a human warmth in the forms of two friendly Japanese nurses who turned up at the Swimming Club to upset the routine of our swims.

At first we could not make them out, for they looked like any other Chinese except that they were dressed in western clothes, something not so common at that time in Penang.

We saw them even as we were turning round at the far end to return towards the club. So we continued our swim back towards the club end of the pool without thinking further on the subject.

When we reached the end of the pool, they had disappeared from the railings. Then, as we climbed the steps out of the pool, we suddenly saw them again, right in front of us and excitedly speaking in Japanese. They were two prettily dressed Japanese ladies, too young and pretty to be expected at a war front so far away from Japan especially unescorted. Despite their forwardness and unconcerned attitude, our reaction was understandably defensive and cautious. They were Japanese who had defeated the British and therefore had a right to be on the premises which now belonged to them. We were but young men who were little more than trespassers and the haunting figure of the *Kempeitai* filled our minds with some apprehension.

But they were smiling. We had never seen a Japanese woman smile, after all we had never met any Japanese women in our lives. As a matter of fact they were not only smiling but speaking to us and gesticulating excitedly at the same time.

This put us, somewhat, at our ease. No hostile women would smile and speak at the same time. But they were speaking in Japanese, obviously taking us for Japanese men. I quickly explained that we were not Japanese but Chinese. At that time, remember, there was no such thing as a Malayan or Malaysian, the nation had not yet come into being. We had no other identity to change to, as if it would have made any difference.

I spoke in English because I thought it was an internationally understood means of communication. It was. One of them, the prettier one who could speak the language better, began then to speak to us in broken and not so easily understood English. But it was understandable.

They were nurses, she explained. It was a very matter of fact introduction. They had come to Penang and would be here for a short while. They wanted to see if there was a place where they could swim. They were happy to have found the club and the swimming pool and glad to have seen us. But they could not swim. Could we teach them how to swim? They had swimming costumes in the club and they could change into them.

They had little sophistication and their forthright style of speaking made it easy to make out that they were obviously happy to have met us. All hesitancy and caution overcome, perhaps overtaken by the male instinct, I agreed. Perhaps, too, I realised that it would have been foolish to turn them down when there was this opportunity to make friends with a Japanese.

Teong Kooi was more cautious. What if the *Kempeitai* caught us fraternising with unescorted young Japanese women in a swimming pool by the sea, he asked. I thought otherwise. In the first place, no one ever came to the pool and in any event, with the Japanese women explaining what we were doing, it was possible that we might widen the protective screen around us.

There was a hurried discussion between them and then she turned round to us and asked us to wait, signalling for us to sit down by the side of the pool.

Imagine my mixed feelings. They were Japanese women and we were only locals. Perhaps if we kept to the swimming pool and, in that way, remained in "neutral" territory we would stay out of trouble. He agreed. But then, why take risks? On the other hand, why run away?

Was it maleness? Was it sex? What was it? Just friendliness? Or was it escapism? They had indicated no promises.

Once Teong Kooi had overcome his initial reluctance, he was ever willing to display his prowess, for he was a good swimmer, with an athletic figure. Without the identity of their uniforms, they looked little different from our Chinese girls. They looked like two ordinary young women looking for something to take away the boredom of having no friends in a strange country. They were not so strange after all. Soon we had to keep reminding ourselves that they were Japanese and if anything should happen to them, it would not be our policemen asking questions but the *Kempeitai*.

Thus began a short and what might have been an idyllic south sea interlude, for we were on a tropical island with the sun and a tropical shore, had it not been for the war and the fact that we were an occupied people in an occupied land.

The innocence of our meeting, the absence of the military and the absence of the feeling of war brought about a sense of escapade as if some feeling of romance was enough to warm the friendship.

As we became more familiar, the war faded more into the background and the friendship became personal and unrelated to nationalism. We soon lost the awareness that they were from an enemy nation. The swimming pool became full of fun as innocent laughter began to resound in it. Even the pointing of fingers became less and less as we grew more instinctive in our understanding of what we were trying to say to one another.

In next to no time at all, despite our language difficulties, we were already fraternising, if such a word can be applied to friendships between colonial subjects and civilians of the occupying race. What bound us together was probably boredom mixed with romanticism, their reason for meeting us in the first place being no longer relevant.

We first taught them how to float, then to paddle and, as soon as they could keep afloat, we taught them how to swim. In the beginning, we occupied the shallow end of the pool so no one would drown. Then, we slowly went deeper and deeper as they began to swim.

It was a beautiful escapade. Not in the usual sense of the word, for the escapade was from the tension of the war and the *Kempeitai*, for even their image slowly faded from our minds.

They were free on the weekends and would come on Saturday and Sunday late in the afternoon and leave for their home and dinner. This would leave us some two hours together each time we met. It was understandable that we began to feel at ease enough for one of them to suggest that we not swim in the pool but in the sea where there was a platform and a diving board.

That was much more fun. The pool was open to anyone who wanted to stop and look down from the road. We sometimes felt uncomfortable at the thought that someone might spy on us and let on that there were two Chinese youths swimming in the Swimming Club with two Japanese women.

So their request was met with enthusiasm by me and with another bout of questions from Teong Kooi. Did I not think swimming in the pool was much better? What if the *Kempeitai* should find us on the beach? Would it be safe? How could we explain?

The beach was below the club and shaded by the club and the trees. It was cooler, more secluded and there was more privacy. Unless one came into the club and looked down over the railings we would not be seen. On the other hand, if we went out to the platform, it would be too far to know the identity of the swimmers. There was sufficient reason to accept their suggestion. So down we went to the beach and the sea.

In that situation, our friendship cemented quickly. But there was always the shadow of the *Kempeitai* between us which stopped us venturing further. What if they should drown in the sea? The drowning of a Japanese woman, not to speak of a Japanese nurse, was bound to provoke investigation and almost incarceration by the *Kempeitai*, no matter how accidental it was. Should any one of them venture too far away from the shore, she would be ordered back to shore.

But whenever we went to the shore and too close to the trees, even in their shadows in the setting sun, the idea of being found by the *Kempeitai* in close proximity to young unattached Japanese women sent us scrambling back into the sea.

So, in the end, it was no better than if we had been in the pool. We could only swim in waist deep water, not too close to the shore and not too far into the sea. It was much safer that way, but less adventurous. It was not a friendship with sexual overtones. But then, at that time, Freud and the sexual libido was not yet in vogue. It had not even come to Penang if it did reach Japan.

Though it might seem strange today, the mores and the customs then were such that sex did not take a free and predominant position as it does today in friendships. Teong Kooi, particularly, was more conventional than I was. In fact, he joined the police force after the war and became a member of the Special Branch before he became a police prosecutor in the court. I wonder, if anything had taken place without his approval, he would have blown the proverbial whistle and put up his hand to cry halt. Even proximity seemed to him to be already too proximate.

In many ways, those were happy days, enlightening days. We had not expected to meet Japanese women. It was our first introduction to foreign women and to their ways. I had thought that young Japanese women were not exposed to socialism and they stayed at home after their marriage. Because we had never had Japanese friends before, comparisons were inevitable. We mentally compared them with our local girls. They looked nearly the same but they were from a temperate country so they were more ruddy, more stocky and firmer. There was a bloom on their skins where there was none on ours.

Physically, there was little difference. Mentally too, there was little basic difference. Most young men and women had similar demands and characteristics. But there the similarities ended, if there was little difference in physical appearance and basic demands, there were cultural differences brought about by religion and social customs.

Nevertheless, I have often wondered if our friendship could have blossomed further had we understood more of the Japanese language and custom and had the shadow of the *Kempeitai* not stood in between and had the relationship lasted longer.

One Saturday, the inevitable happened and they came to tell us that they had received instructions to prepare for their departure from Penang and that they had come to say goodbye.

They had received orders to report for duty. Where they were going to they did not say. Thus ended a brief strange friendship of the war. We never saw them again.

But late that Sunday afternoon, as we were leaving the pool, as if by way of recompense, the caretaker asked if we could come to the club on Monday evening. He would be giving us a surprise, he said. But we had to be there before six in the evening and we had to be on time. Why, he did not say.

That afternoon, we turned up at six. He was not ready, he told us. We had to go for a swim in the sea as he was emptying the pool. True enough, the pool was nearly empty. He would give us a dinner, he said.

We went off for our swim. About an hour later he called out to us from the verandah, to come up to the pool. When we came up, he gave us a pail and a scoop each and pointed at the quickly emptying pool, normally so clean and sparkling.

Now it still looked clean, the water was knee deep at the shallow end, but it was no longer sparkling but bubbling.

Prawns, he said, pointing out at the froth. We looked hard. Then we saw some things jumping in the midst of the froth. Prawns, he repeated.

We looked again. Then I saw an amazing sight. Impossible, fully grown prawns up to the size of three inches long jumping up here and there to escape the ever shallowing pool.

Where on earth did the prawns come from? The swimming pool was full of them, the swimming pool filled with filtered sea water, the swimming pool that had always seemed so sparkling clean. It was impossible that the pool was a breeding pond. Yet it was.

The eggs of the prawn were of such a size that they could not be filtered out and had filled the pool with the sea water and the plankton in the water multiplying in the sun had allowed them to mature in a period of only two months.

At first I could not believe my eyes. The very pool seemed to be seething with life. Then, as we were about to wade into the fast emptying pool, Teong Kooi drew my attention to a more amazing sight.

"Snake," he cried, pointing at an even more amazing sight. In the midst of the jumping prawns something was moving through the water in swift spurts, dashing here and there.

It was an octopus, said the caretaker. I hesitated for a second or so and then I decided to enter the pool for it. I was not sure but the way it spurted in swift succession persuaded me that it could not be a snake. Snakes would swim, not spurt. An octopus or a squid would be more likely to do so.

Then I saw a long thin shape which my curiosity compelled me to catch. It turned out to be a baby octopus, measuring four feet across when finally captured and fully stretched.

The fact that it could only have come into the pool as an egg fascinated me.

That evening, the caretaker prepared our meal. He had made provision for four of us but, sadly, there were only two. As I ate my way through the huge plate of prawns, flavoured by the chilli sauce to go with it, my mind was not with the two girls, as if there was a touch of sadness in the air. Somehow, my mind went back again and again to the amazing discovery of the fact the prawns could be carried into ponds and fed themselves on plankton to be ready for harvesting in two months.

If prawn eggs which can be carried in by the sea and could hatch and grow in a swimming pool without human intervention, how much more of a harvest we could get with feeding them, provided that oxygen and fresh sea water could be used to replenish the pond at every high tide through a system of sluice gates.

If that was not the inspiration for prawn breeding after the war in Taiwan, it was at least the inspiration that made me set up my first pool for prawn breeding during the war.

Between Bayan Lepas airport and the sea was a huge stretch of mangrove swamps interspersed with pools here and there. Supposing I could isolate one of the shallower pools and keep the sea water in and replenish it by a sluice gate, which I could carefully open during high tides, surely I could get a regular crop of prawns every two months? Could I not then have a prawn farm that was naturally fed and which would cost little?

I put my plans into practice later when I turned a piece of mangrove swamp into a pool with a sluice gate through which to replenish the pool with fresh seawater during high tides. I worked with a family which had gone up to Bayan Lepas at the outbreak of war. It was a Saw family and Teochew.

It was a good idea. It was a success as far as the breeding was concerned. But sea otters came. It was unexpected and had not been anticipated. Otters could scent fish and prawns from miles away and it seemed that a school of them had come all the way across the channel.

Their uncanny sense of smell led them to the pool and we would see a few swimming around the pool making short work of the prawns. We could not carry guns and when their presence was discovered, traps and netting were put around the pond. They avoided the traps and burrowed under the nets and continued to divest the pool of its prawns. The project was abandoned. The idea was a success but the project was a failure.

But there was a baby otter which was caught and I took it home to keep as a memento and a pet till it developed a habit of going for the toes of anyone going through the kitchen to the toilet at nights so that I had finally to let it go where I had found it. It promptly disappeared and was never to be seen again.

Often, after I had returned from England I would pass by the area and my mind would go wander back to those days and I would wonder what had happened to the two Japanese nurses. Had it not been for them, the breeding of prawns might not have taken place and my ideas of the Japanese might have still been a distorted one. I had lost contact with them, I had failed in my experiment, but then what is victory or defeat, success or failure, when everything winds up in the dust; the purpose is lost when the need is also lost. But what I have gained is what had helped me to mature, that is all.

Let us not face the winter winds
Or to wear our hearts in our faces
But let us cover up our souls and
The warmth within with scarves.

And do not let the cold hard blade
Of winter's hug chill your breath
Or the cold hard blades of frost
Cut off the hidden buds of spring.

20. THE EPOSHO

IT was now becoming obvious that even if a war was planned, whether we would win it or not was a bit of a gamble. As for individuals like us, we were caught in the war. We did not choose it. How we should act in it, was often not our choice and many of us could only react to the war as it found us. This was true of friend or foe.

No deliberate decision put us where we were, even if we were free to choose; for circumstances often made decisions for us if the state did not. We did not know how the nurses came to be nurses and whether they were conscripts or not. Nor did they choose to come to Penang.

As for ourselves, we did not plan ever to meet them. It was the jelly fish that sent us to the Penang Swimming Club and chance found us there at the same time. So we had come to meet them by chance. But was it chance and was it due to a series of accidents? This becomes speculative even if Buddha had said it was *karma* and could have been due to our relationship in an earlier life. How this should have come about is a matter of speculation.

This was even more so with Professor Kirita and Yamagata, both of whom belonged to the new generation of non-militarists. They did not conceive Greater East Asia Co-prosperity Sphere. Professor Kirita was an economics teacher and Yamagata was a newly graduated economics student.

But they were called up for service of their motherland and put in charge of the Eposho which was supposed to be a goodwill organisation to foster goodwill between the public and the Japanese military. It was doubtful even if they had anything to do with the concept even if they had to run the organisation.

I came only to be present at the inaugural meeting because I happened to be stopped on my way to my workshop from my firm of importers and exporters and wholesalers in Prangin Road on my newly acquired Ariel 500 which I had purchased from someone who had managed to keep it off the road when the Japanese came to the island because he was afraid that it might be taken away.

But the Japanese did not seem interested in motorcycles so I thought it was safe and purchased it for use of the garage I had set up. It was chance which enabled him to sell off a machine that he could not use. It was by chance that I had bought it. But though chance played a great deal in my life, it was not by chance that I was chosen to be a member of the Eposho. Someone must have suggested my name except that I am not sure who, for I was selected and the Japanese did not know enough to select me. There were many relatives and others who could have been picked.

Heah Hock Khoon was a school friend who was to become the Chairman of the Rubber Growers Association after the war. He seemed excited. There was an excitement in his voice when he informed me that I was wanted by "the Japanese" who were at that moment waiting for me in the premises of the Chinese Rice Merchants' Association then in Macalister Road, now torn down to become a hotel and a complex.

He could not tell me why I was wanted. He was as much in the dark as I was. But, from his manner, it was clear that I should not refuse. Still in the dark, I followed him to the meeting where I found some twenty or so other local personalities who seemed equally nonplused and somewhat in fear, all waiting for my presence for the meeting to start.

The building where we met and which became the office of the Eposho, has now been torn down to become the Agora Hotel. It was not a grand building. It was not worth preserving. Nor were we a happy lot.

This was the inaugural meeting of the Eposho. Heading it was Professor Kirita, a civilian and an economics professor in Japan assisted by the younger Yamagata, newly graduated from university, also a civilian. Present were the head of the *Kempeitai*, General Terata, from their headquarters in Taiping, and the chief of the naval base in Penang, Captain Hidaka with his deputy, Commander Hatta, a jovial and well-built man.

But, since the Eposho was to be a liaison and a complaints body receiving most complaints from the civilians, I wonder if it was a good idea to let General Terata loose on us.

It was Yamagata who addressed the meeting because Professor Kirita did not have such a good command of English. It was only a short address but it served to dispel the disquiet I could see in the local faces round the table. For the meeting was not to get at anyone which was the first impression when we saw the military personnel.

It was a sort of reconciliation committee. The Eposho was to cement friendship with the people, a mutual benefit society. Its main job was to receive complaints from us about excesses of the military so action could be taken to redress wrongs.

No sooner was the address over and we had adjourned for tea when the questions started. Everyone wanted to know how his name was chosen. No one knew. Everyone said he had received a phone call to be present and no one would name the caller who obviously had to be one of us present.

Behind the polite smiles was universal suspicion and reserve. In my case, I told them that it was Hock Khoon who had stopped me on the road. He was quick to point out that he had been asked to look for me that very morning when he had come to the office of the Eposho earlier. So that was that. It remains a mystery to me till today.

We were an odd collection. There was little in common between us. Our ages ranged from that of my uncle down to me; it spanned a generation. Some of them were millionaires, such as my uncle and Choong Eng Hye. Some were scions of millionaires such as Loh Hoot Yeang, Soon Cheng Sun and Tan Lip Sun. Some were prominent people such as Koh Sin Hock, the comprador of an English Bank but of no particular fortune and then there was Dr Ong Chong Kheng, a middle-aged doctor of high political expectation but not of any particular revolutionary fervour.

The rest, some of whom I cannot recall, were very young men such as Heah Hock Khoon with myself who seemed to be the youngest and most nondescript.

The only thing we had in common was that we were all Chinese. There seemed to be no good logic in the selection.

My uncle, for example, was a recluse and seemed to have retired from active business. There was no reason for him to change his ways or thinking. Koh Sin Hock, slightly younger, was middle class and a comprador of an English bank with hardly any independent and political mind. Choong Eng Hye was also a millionaire but with independent ways and no real political awareness. Loh Hoot Yeang came from Cambridge and was interested in only minding his own business. So also with most of the rest. They were hardly men suitable to lead the population into new ways, much less support the Japanese war effort. This was another reason for us to revise our initial suspicion that there could have been a political point behind the organisation.

Since the character of the membership was hardly identifiable politically or suitable for political work, the Eposho could hardly be a political body. Well, that was a good start.

If it was correct that we would act as members of a complaints committee, it would also be a waste of time, since the organisation had no executive power or any teeth to bite. That was also a blessing, for we could antagonise no one.

There was no other equivalent anywhere within Japanese occupied territory. Nothing like it existed anywhere else in Malaya or Singapore. We thought that perhaps the idea came from the British-nominated local councils which existed in Penang before the war and that the Japanese must have thought to imitate them.

But even then, it was a non-starter. The British councils consisted of executive members of the British administrative services, the executive arm of the local government which met every so often to confirm or deny departmental decisions.

They were dominated by the executive departmental heads with executive power. Even their Presidents were senior officers with great experience.

But the Eposho had no such executives nor had it any power. Professor Kirita and Yamagata were not civil service officers. One was a professor of economics whilst the other was but a new economics graduate and both of them had no civil service training or experience.

It could only be a talk shop. Complaints, if any, would generally centre around the *Kempeitai*, the navy kept much to themselves, and who would have the courage to complain about the *Kempeitai* to its own head who would usually be present at every meeting.

General Tarata may have been a nice man. But his post in the *Kempeitai* precluded all attempts to be close to him. We saw him as a taciturn no nonsense man and believed that the *Kempeitai*, having taken the freedom and lives of so many men, could not but have someone equally callous to be in command. To make complaint to him of his own men required great courage.

Captain Hidaka was a different kettle of fish altogether. He was a much-travelled naval man, always smiling and at ease. But his naval men hardly came into contact with civilians. He was so pleasant that there was a strong rumour that Penang did not suffer so much from the excesses of the *Kempeitai* because the navy was in charge of the island.

Whether that was true, we do not know. But Hidaka gave us the impression that his job was with the navy and battles at sea and civilian matters were not the concern of the navy. We were thus quite friendly towards him and did not avoid him.

After a while, the meetings became less and less formal and enthusiastic. They were not even always well attended for those who had any good excuse at all, would avoid coming to the meeting and quite a few of those who turned up, such as my uncle, would have nothing to say.

But a lot of goodwill was personally generated by Professor Kirita and Yamagata due to personal friendships that developed between us. The fact that, never once, during the war, had they even asked for women, was something that gave us confidence in them.

They did not agree with the war and they did not like any power nor had they the will to exert any power. I suspect that all Professor Kirita, the elder of the two, a small man who constantly blinked through his glasses in a bemused sort of way, looking as if he was waiting for you to finish what you had to say before running back to his room and his books, wanted was to return to his university. He was certainly a misfit in the theatre of war.

Yamagata was a different person altogether. A romantic with strong ideas of his own, he did not hesitate to voice his anti-war feelings. But that did not relate to his duties which he performed with great enthusiasm.

He was always against the war and wanted it to end so he could carry on with his life. It was what we also wanted, but no one could be sure if he wanted it to end the way we wanted it. I suppose I can say that he was in many ways like one of our young men. We all wanted the war to end but to our advantage. But principally, I think, all he seemed to want was to get out of it and go on with his life.

But as a complaints committee, the Eposho was helpful to me on one occasion when I lost my motorbike to an unknown Japanese who took away my motorbike from where I had left it in front of a coffeeshop.

It was the Ariel 500 I had purchased from the proud owner who had hidden it away for fear of losing it the way I did. I suppose he was right and I was wrong. For that was exactly how I lost it.

But the Japanese who took it was unfortunate. On discovery of the loss, I reported the loss at once to Yamagata. The time for pillage was long past.

Yamatagata told Kirita who phoned the navy who instructed the ferry master to stop whoever might be taking the bike over to the mainland where it was certain to be lost forever.

The luckless Japanese, whose identity I never knew, was stopped at the pier itself and he was told to leave the bike there where I recovered it some two hours after I received a call at the Eposho to go recover the bike at the ferry terminal from the master. It was there, by the side of the ramp waiting for me.

I did not see anyone but the ferry master. I was, again, lucky. I do not know what happened to the thief, but I am sure they did not cut off his head as they had done to the two youths suspected of looting earlier.

The open personalities of Kirita and Yamagata were helpful in another way. Indirectly, they showed us that most civilians were the same, Japanese or enemy. I suppose, being fellow Asians of the same stock, helped us to understand them more.

It is often said that there is no better way to know a society and culture than to become friends with one of their women. The Japanese nurses who had befriended us had given us quite a good picture of the similarity between our cultures between their women and ours. But that was about all.

It was knowing Kirita and Yamagata that was the more important. It was they who allowed the few of us, the younger members of the Eposho, a glimpse of Japanese life at home and who gave us a taste of Japanese culture. They it was who allowed us to go into their home in the evenings (it was the former home of the manager of the Chartered Bank in Western Road, now torn down to become the Heritage Club) where they lived as lonely bachelors.

Hock Khoon, Lip Sun and Cheng Sun were among those like myself who were exposed to their more intimate moments and to learn from them how to imbibe their *sake* and to prepare *sukiyaki* and to partake of raw fish with them.

Putting aside their nationality, it was difficult to think of them as "the enemy" or those from "the other side". There were so many things we could share outside of the war, so many things we had in common, that we were more private individuals than nationalities.

This was true especially with Yamagata who was more of our age group. We had the same kind of sentiments, feelings and attitudes.

But as nationals of Japan, we always felt there was a line between us. This line was the line of duty. This was where such common things as loyalty and national duty had different applications between us and them. It was a barrier that never quite disappeared. We were not all that close.

As we met more Japanese, the cultural differences, complexities and the social structures became more apparent, forcing us to rethink and redefine many of the cliches and the meanings of many terms whose definitions I had taken for granted.

For one thing, I saw that generalisations did not necessarily apply to individuals; that on the individual level, friendships could be formed even if their nations were at war. Though we were at war and I did not agree with Japan, I had no quarrel with the individual Japanese just as they had no personal quarrel with me. But that was only on an individual and personal level and not on a national level.

Secondly, the conduct of war was based on national principles which need not correspond to that on the personal level.

Finally, as we are both individuals and nationals our duties and loyalties do conflict and therefore war limits friendships, no matter how close we are. That is the tragedy of war.

What struck me most about Kirita and Yamagata was their self assurance and their resoluteness. They gave the impression that the Japanese were people of great discipline, capable of great hardships for their nation.

Their discipline, resoluteness and their obedience to duty were often at great cost to themselves. They gave them a sense of loneliness and frustration which often emerged in the sad nostalgia to be found in the songs they love to sing with their *sake* after dinner. It seemed to be a form of escape. It was as if only in their songs could they find release from their suppression and control.

It was this sense of loneliness and suffering that helped us understand that they too, were a suffering people, unlike the happy and carefree sun-drenched people from the warm lands. This, strangely, helped to soften the harshness of the military regime.

We were getting bored with attending meeting after meeting with nothing unusual ever coming up when at one meeting, Yamagata announced that Japan wanted platinum and that they were prepared to pay for it with rice.

Platinum, we understood, was used in settings for jewellery. Somehow they had come to know that the Chinese women in Penang kept jewellery for investment and security for rainy days.

Most of the richer women had jewellery but platinum was rarer than gold which the women preferred because platinum looks like stainless steel.

The offer of rice in exchange was tempting. One could not eat platinum but one could eat rice. The search had begun. For a brief period, goldsmiths were busy melting down jewellery instead of making them.

For a while I stood idly by as this went on. My mother did not believe in jewellery, a burglary long ago having put her off, and I knew no one who had any. For a moment I stood idly by wondering if anyone would want to sell their rice. Then an idea struck me.

Through visits to the junkyards for lorry parts, I had come across a fair amount of old discarded platinum points used in distributors of motor vehicles.

I was not sure if they were made of pure platinum or if they were platinum at all though they were called platinum points. To make sure, I approached Yamagata to find out who would be checking on the platinum and how it was done.

He showed me how it was done. It was a simple enough test. All one had to do was to rub off some of the platinum onto a piece of black stone slate and if the colour changed or fizzled away, it was not platinum. If it did not, it was.

I got hold of a piece of platinum point and experimented at home. I took it to the Eposho the next day. It passed the test. I was in business.

It was so simple that I was afraid that someone would discover this and beat me to it if I was not fast enough. Most probably a Japanese might turn up with a van and pick them all up.

Whilst the others were busy looking secretly for the elusive platinum settings in jewellery, I was soon also secretly working quickly and quietly at home.

All I had to do was to melt the platinum off the points recovered from the junkyards with a bunsen burner at night in an earthen crucible and collect the little lumps after they had sufficiently cooled down. Slowly, little by little, a small piece at a time, I began to exchange my unwanted platinum for precious rice.

Soon the junkyards were denuded of these otherwise useless points.

To this day I do not know if the platinum I sold was the right stuff and if they worked for I had by then guessed they wanted the platinum for platinum points themselves.

It was not actually within my scheme of things. I did not plan it. Had I not been compelled to assemble lorries, I might not have known that such things as platinum points existed and that they contained platinum. I had been compelled to become a mechanic and this was my reward. Without it I might never have obtained such a simple and cheap source of rice.

My rice brought about a great deal of surprise at home even if it was not much. We were already eating *ragi*, a millet, and tapioca at that time, supplementing it with rationed rice. What I found in the junkyard was not really that much but it was a godsend. Since I had nowhere else to put the rice, I put it in one of the empty rooms in the servant's quarters. But I had forgotten another squirrel. She was in the form of my mother. One day I thought to check the stock when, to my surprise, I discovered that a few of the gunny sacks that contained them were looking slimmer than usual. I asked my mother about it and she suggested that the rats must have been busy.

Not happy with her answer, for it was clear that someone had been filching as rats do not extract rice without leaving holes in the gunny sacks, I confronted our cook, an old retainer. In self-defence, he came out with the truth.

My mother was the culprit. She had used a rice extractor, consisting of a sharpened iron pipe, and had given some of the rice to her impoverished friends, no doubt also benefiting some of the few informers we discovered after the war who were in the habit of visiting us.

It made my mother happy to do it and she was not taking much. There was plenty left for our small family. It was not of great consequence. So, as long as she was happy, I was also happy. I let the matter rest. But I never let on that I knew what she had been doing. Such was the luck of the game imposed by God on us.

*We cannot plan for everything in war
The unexpected happens. A carbuncle,
War emits poisons and must erupt
To emit poisons before it kills itself.
Pantomimes and ephemeral dreams
Of little meaning, come with treachery
And wild deliriums of grandeur,
To leave behind worthless, crippled things.*

21. WAR'S A CARBUNCLE

DR McKern was a Scottish doctor who loved the island and had made a fortune before the war. He lived alone though he was a well-known gynecologist who had delivered many babies on the island.

He was well known, liked and had enough to build himself a huge house on top of a small rise overlooking the North channel with a beautiful view of Kedah Peak. He was in want of nothing. Because he loved the island, he decided to put in a secret cellar where he thought he would spend his time should the Japanese war take place.

He had foreseen the war. He was right. The war came. He took refuge in his cellar and trusted only one person with his secret, I think it was a driver. He thought he would be safe there.

Here, fate, or *karma*, took over. The war took longer than he expected. Finding his self-enforced imprisonment irksome after a while and getting impatient, he developed the habit of coming out of his shelter once in a while to taste the midnight air along the beach.

Soon, rumours began to spread that a white ghost could be seen on the beach near his house on some nights which aroused the curiosity of the Japanese.

The Japanese were not superstitious and sent a search party to look for this mysterious white man who was supposed to be a ghost and he was shortly afterwards discovered by the Japanese.

It was only shortly before the end of the war that he was discovered and there were rumours that he was exposed by the driver. Whether this was true or not, no one lived to tell the tale.

He was right to foresee the war but wrong to think he would not be discovered by the Japanese who carted him off to a prison camp. He did not return after the war and we presume he must have died in the camp. Why he should have been taken to prison is odd if you think that he had already detained himself in his cellar and meant no harm to anyone. One would have thought that a prison camp is for enemies one feared would cause harm.

Was this *karma* or was it betrayal that he should have thought to remain in this country to be detained and to lose his beautiful home? Or was it betrayal by someone out of fear for his life, for we are not sure how the Japanese came to discover his secret hideout.

This does happen even to friends. Betrayals by our own friends through fear was not uncommon during the war. Such an instance happened to me.

It might have led to a most serious consequence had I not been lucky. Fortunately, little harm came of it.

When I became a member of the Eposho, the clerk of the organisation was a school friend. Whilst there, he quickly struck up a close relationship with another co-worker whom he was to marry.

One morning, I thought to be nice to them and invited them for morning coffee in a coffeeshop above the Penang Road market, the approach of which was by a staircase to the side and back of the market.

When we were about to finish our drinks, as luck would have it, what appeared to be a Japanese worker in naval uniform came up the stairs into the coffeeshop with a friend, also in uniform. They walked past us to occupy a table next to ours. There were with me this couple and another friend who was with me when I invited them.

But as he was about to sit down, his roving eye was taken by the sight of this pretty girlfriend of my friend. He seemed to change his mind, straighten himself and came over to our table and began speaking in Japanese.

His ultimate intention became obvious after he had posed a few questions at us. Were we from the *Kempeitai*? He began. When I answered in the negative, he went on to the next question. Were we from the army? No, again I shook my head. We knew no Japanese but by then we knew the names of all the Japanese organisations. As he went down the list of these Japanese organisations to which I kept repeating in the negative, he became more and more agitated and began to raise his voice.

No sooner had he finished the whole list of Japanese organisations including that of the Gunseikanbu, meaning the Japanese civil administration and discovered that we were no more than ordinary private persons, he reached over the table and grabbed my friend's girlfriend by her hand and began to pull her to his table. Perhaps he thought she was a waitress or knew she was a customer. Whatever it was he should not have done that. At the sight of what he was trying to do, I lost my temper and my valour came before my discretion.

I got up, my reaction coming spontaneously. Pushing my chair backwards, I got up to have some elbow room and pulled his hands away from her. He let the girl go and turned his attention on me, raising his hand to strike at me.

Before I realised it I had reached for his hand and pulled him forward, unbalancing him. As he stumbled forward, I suddenly let him go so he would fall forward. He did but recovered his balance, reached for his cane chair and lifted it to hit me with it.

But even as he did that, I had pulled it toward me and, as he resisted the pull, thrust it back at him so that he fell backwards and across his table.

At that moment, his friend rose from his seat. I made a move towards him and he changed his mind and quickly sat down again. There was some hesitation on their part, the reason becoming only clear later on, and before they could recover, I thought it was time to beat a retreat and quickly signalled to my friends to leave.

As we got up to go, the man staggered to his feet. But, to my surprise, he made no further attempt to do anything further but merely recovered his chair to sit down.

As we reached the stairs, thinking I could confuse them into thinking I was a Japanese, I turned back to them and let loose the two swear words I knew in Japanese.

As it turned out, I was fortunate on this account. He was no Japanese but a Korean port worker, a colonial like myself. And there the matter should have rested. But the matter did not stop there.

That afternoon, around four, Commander Hatta, whom I had seen at the Eposho with Captain Hidaka and who sometimes stood in for him, the second in command to Captain Hidaka, his red flag fluttering from the bonnet of his car, came slowly into the grounds of the house and stopped at the porch to look for me. I was at home and could not excuse myself from the short ride he offered.

To strike someone in Japanese uniform, he explained to me when we were in the car, was a serious matter. It was punishable by death and I should not have done what I did.

I willingly admitted that what I had done was serious. It was better than to argue. Besides, I had to placate him before I came out with my excuse. It was that, to me, rape or attempted rape was something disgraceful to any army. It should be resisted, if only to maintain the dignity of the Japanese. And I might even do it again, I explained, for it gave a bad impression of the Imperial Japanese army.

I am not sure if he took the bait and accepted what I said. Or, I doubt, in view of what was happening, that I would do it again. I must admit that my heart was racing even if I did try to look adamant and, insulted.

I went on to soften my crime by explaining that I had intervened not to insult anyone, much less the Japanese uniform, but more to save the dignity and the honour of the military. If anything had happened to the girl, a bad image might have been created.

I went on to say that it was the man who struck out at me. All I had done was in self-defence when he raised his hand and then his chair to strike at me, ending my defence with the statement that action should be taken against the man rather than me.

Hatta switched off. For a while he said nothing. When he opened up again, he merely said I had been lucky that I had struck at a Korean and not a Japanese, but he was in a Japanese uniform and it should not happen again.

Then, as if suddenly making up his mind to end the matter, to my immense relief, he asked his driver to turn the car back and to take me home. Was it fate that the officer who came to interview me was a nice Japanese who knew me? Was it chance, or *karma*?

Whether action was later taken against the man I do not know, but I was off the hook. I was lucky but I could have got into trouble and I was determined to find out how this incident came to be reported to the navy so quickly.

Now that I knew the man to be a Korean, I had the feeling that the complaint could not have come from him. He would have been happy to let the matter rest for reporting could equally have put him in hot water. It had to be someone closer to home.

My mind went back to the scene. It had to be one of those persons present who had done the dirty on me. Perhaps it was Heah Hock Khoon who, though he was not present, had many friends who could have told him what had happened and as he was also a member of the Eposho, he could have identified us by our descriptions. But he knew nothing of the incident.

I took a long shot. Even if they were involved, my two friends could have reported the incident to keep themselves out of trouble. This was entirely possible, knowing how timid and self-protective they were.

I was right. When I asked them how the navy had come to know of the incident so quickly, they immediately confessed.

On their return they had discussed the matter between themselves and come to the conclusion that if the man reported the matter before them, the matter could be twisted and they might get into trouble themselves. Since they were innocent, they thought that the best defence was to tell the truth at once.

They could not find me to discuss the matter and time was all important. But, they insisted, they told the truth and had said that the man had accosted the woman and I had come to their defence and had beaten the man off.

Of course, I was indignant. In fact, I was very angry. Nor was it quite correct to say I had beaten the man off or that I had even struck at him. I had, to my mind, only warded off the blow of the man.

But that was a nicety. The least they could have done was to forewarn me or at least agreed to take concerted action. The least they could have done was to thank me instead of sneaking on me.

If they were such cowards, they should not have gone out with me. They were apologetic and conciliatory. Their only defence was fear. It was fear for themselves that had caused them to make the report. They did not forewarn me because I was not to be found. They had no intention to harm me.

Their excuses and their rationalisation were normal. That was what most people would do. What could I say? Was that not the reason most people give for their actions?

It was fortunate that it was the navy and Hatta had personally come to verify the truth. So, it was a friend and his girlfriend who had let me down. But I let the matter drop. There was no point holding on to my anger. The least I could do was not to stretch out my neck in future.

I did not bring it up again, not with my friends, not with Kirita who had said nothing about the incident to me though it was he who must have carried the matter to the navy. One cannot depend on anyone.

Such was the nature of war. I had learned another lesson. There are limits to what friends can do. Like in all matters of danger, one had to learn to depend only on oneself.

Was it fated, luck or was it *karma* that the person I had struck was a Korean and that he was under the jurisdiction of Captain Hidaka that had saved me?

In war it is God who disposes.
We can only plan, propose and hope
To survive the unexpected. A carbuncle,
War must discharge deluding poisons,
Produce delirious pantomimes of grandeur
Fabricate wild dreams of nonsense,
To leave behind worthless, crippled things.

22. THAT WE MAY SURVIVE

I COME from a family of professionals. I did not understand trading with its emphasis on profit and loss as its main, if not the only, motive and purpose of the trader or the businessman. I now had to enter this strange world of the businessman where sophistry and argument were kept at a minimum.

There was never any question as to the right or wrong of things. As long as it was profitable, within one's capacity and in the line of one's business, and as long as one did not come into conflict with the law, it was done. This was made simpler by the war where survival made irrelevant things more irrelevant.

To survive I had begun as a sundry shopkeeper. But, having become one, its limitations began to be irksome for there is little intellectuality in such a trade. Dealing in rationed items was easy. I soon found it boring and I wanted to stretch my wings, so to speak.

I thought I would venture into something bigger, more challenging, something that would also allow me the excuse of leaving the island from time to time to feel what it was like in the world outside. That was why I started to set up my import and export firm before the edict upset my calculations.

So, as soon as I had put the danger of being despatched to the mainland behind me by establishing a workshop and registering myself as a mechanic, I returned to my earlier plan which had been so rudely interrupted.

My plans had the same purport, not so much to make profits, but to make sure that we would not starve during the war. I knew that our local staple foods came from Kedah, Thailand, Burma and Indonesia before the war. But Burma, which provided us with most of our rice, and Indonesia had been cut off by the war. Only Kedah and Thailand remained.

To travel out of the island was a risk at a time when the Japanese were in the habit of looking for Communist agents on board the trains. It was a risk but an exciting one for a youth and being an importer and exporter gave a good excuse for travelling.

I did not have enough to start my business. My profits as a sundry shopkeeper were meagre even if I was already well prepared for surviving the war. For the capital required, I had to approach my uncle Cheng Teik, a property magnate and a millionaire who had a soft spot for my mother though he was not on amicable terms with my father.

The premises of my firm, Kean Swee, was right next to the Prangin Road market which was at the end of the bombing area and the Chinese wholesale business world run mostly by the Teochews. It was convenient as it was within two hundred yards of my sundry shop in Maxwell Road opposite my father's old mansion and within the area of the Chinese business world.

This was the world of the Chinese-educated, living in a universe of their own and in which the English environment was almost unknown and whose norms and ethics I never knew. It was a world with little tolerance for ignorance and any sign of inexperience and rawness was immediately pounced upon and exploited. Truth, *per se*, was stupid. It was subject to the situation and need. One told what one should tell and no more and even that must be to one's advantage.

In the world of Chinese business, one expected merciless duplicity and cut-throat skill. It is only when one is trusted and is accepted into the fold that one can feel free and relaxed. Once this mutual trust is established, no time is wasted in beating around the bush. At that point, one begins to see what had been barred from outside. One becomes an insider and one begins to know the truth. This was a basic principle on which they worked.

I was lucky on two scores. I quickly found a Teochew manager who was looking for a job. He did most of the sales once I had concluded the purchase and I looked after the banking and payments.

I then found Cho Suan, the eldest in a family of an old firm of importers and wholesalers Chin Teow Hin. We got on famously right from the beginning. He suited me and soon I was eating with his family and his workers in his shop which was a sign that I had been accepted. For it was the custom of such businesses that everyone in the family and the workers ate together. Strangers were invited to the coffeeshops and eating houses nearby, but not to the workshop home, so to speak.

It was because I was not business-inclined that I sometimes mixed business with pleasure, mixing up my motives. This once took me all the way to Singapore shortly into the Occupation. It was, in a way, a mistake. But not quite.

I was anxious to know what had happened to my friends in Singapore after its fall. We had heard a lot of rumours of Japanese atrocities but had no hard news. When I was roped into the Eposho, I had met Lee Siew Gnok, another unwilling member of the Eposho.

I cannot recall meeting him at the first gathering but when I saw him I recalled the occasion just before the outbreak of the war when he was brought to the house by my father, who was his lawyer. He was introduced him to us as an enterprising young man who was something of a Chinese scholar who had learnt how to can food through a correspondence course and had discovered how to can curry, something thought impossible at that time because it contained easily fermented coconut milk.

When I saw him, I at once saw a way how I could visit Singapore to look up some of my friends.

I asked him if he was still canning curry. He was. I pressed him further and asked if he could sell his curry to the Japanese. The Japanese, he told me, did not take curry. They did not want curry and they refused even to touch his stocks of chicken curry he had in his stores when they first came.

I asked if he still had this curry. He had. Would he sell some to me? I did not say what I wanted the curry for.

He had a stock of chicken curry. It was not a prohibited item and provided I could get a permit for export, I could take them anywhere I wished. But was it advisable to travel these days, he cautioned. I just told him I would find out. But I was pretty confident that with a permit and as a trader with a load of eatables which the Japanese did not want, it should not be difficult or so dangerous. That is, if I travelled by train with a defined destination and if I did not leave the train during the stopovers.

Siew Gnok was helpful. A few days later, I was able to meet him in his office with Cho Suan and concluded the deal.

I could not go to Singapore without Cho Suan. He knew the ropes and the market, and he knew a consignee and where he could sell the curry. I knew next to nothing and my contribution was the idea, the enthusiasm and the capital. I did not even know how I could make any profit, only that edibles would find a ready market in Singapore.

He seemed happy with the project but insisted on 50 per cent of the profit, whatever it was. He did not see any difficulty in selling them to his friends in Singapore. Needless to say, they were all Teochews.

But I had difficulty in obtaining the permits. I was given a permit to carry only 240 cases. But the permit did not say how many tins should be in each case. Siow Gnok had said he could let me have 480 cases. I had to think of a way out.

Each case contained 24 tins. I could not carry 480 cases in two hundred and forty. So we decided to double the contents by making bigger cases. They were pinewood cases and it was not difficult to knock up 240 of them to carry 48 tins each. It would be unusual but we might carry it off.

So my first export venture began. It was on this trip that I was to learn how skilful he was and to be amazed at the non-English-speaking world of the Chinese traders.

Amongst the amazing discoveries was when I discovered how the Chinese traders had been able to keep to themselves and manage to survive with little or no contacts with those outside their world.

The Chinese business world had an environment of its own. It required little or no contact at all with the mainstream British business world. The Teochews controlled the sinews of their trade all the way from Bangkok to Singapore. They dealt with Chinese things, with such produce from harvesting the crops to retail sales through a system entirely within their hands. They therefore did not need to have contact with the British business houses and this also meant that they could survive with little Japanese contact for the Japanese were also foreigners who had little knowledge of Chinese trade.

Right from the beginning of our journey, the innovativeness, independence, initiative and difference in the approach to business methods of the Chinese trader were clearly demonstrated.

We had to take the train and accompany the goods. To take the train we had to ferry our consignment over by junk. This meant clearing our export through a customs checkpoint on the side of the island at a jetty designated for such exports.

At the checkpoint, Cho Suan demonstrated his consummate skill. It is the usual custom to pack twenty-four tins to a case, or carton, and should the customs officers wake up to the fact that our cartons contained 48, instead of the usual 24, there could be a problem.

The customs station and office stood on a concrete platform at the water's edge. The unloading from the handcarts to the junk began on the side of the road next to the checkpoint, the junk stood on the other end of the checkpoint by a narrow and short jetty of planks.

The cases had to be carried across the front of the office where stood a few customs officers whilst inside the office at his desk was the duty officer to verify the consignment and stamp his stamp of approval on the permit which we had to carry all the way down to Singapore.

We had to clear all this. Instead of approaching to befriend the duty officer at the desk whilst the goods went through the checkpoint, Cho Suan arranged for an incident which would distract the officer on duty.

He went into the office for the documents and began to ask the duty office for his stamp even before the goods had gone by.

As he spoke and the first of the cases, carried shoulder high, came by, it slipped off the shoulder of its carrier and fell onto the concrete floor, bursting open and spilling its contents which began to scatter across the platform in all directions.

The sight of these tins of chicken curry, a delicacy, was too much for the officers, deprived by the war as we were. Nothing could stop them as they rushed to recover what they could get and to prevent a few of them from rolling into the sea where the tins would be lost to all standing there. It was a quick fix.

When I looked at him, Cho Suan, who made no attempt to restrain them, gave me a wink. It was a deliberate move. As the officers helped themselves, the loading of the junk proceeded smoothly uninterrupted.

In the meanwhile, the customs officers, having recovered what they could and seemingly pleased with themselves, stood by, watching the loading and uncertain if they should return the goods to us or not.

But the case was smashed and we could not repack them; so, why don't they take them for themselves instead of throwing them into the sea? Cho Suan suggested.

Why not? Everyone was happy. We had lost a case but there was still the rest for ourselves. One case out of two hundred and forty was a small discount. After all, the documents had been stamped and no one was worried enough to count the number of tins in each case. And so it was that we were able to go through the customs without causing anyone any problem.

When we arrived in Singapore, I continued to be amazed. It was quite incredible. When we arrived at the terminal and got out of the goods wagon, all we did was to see where the wagon was being shunted to, note its number, and then we were off by a trishaw to his friend's office without further ado.

At the office, we waited for a while for his friend to come to work, as we were too early. When his friend arrived, there was a short discussion and he handed his friend our permit and the other documents and then we were off to our hotel which his friend's staff had, in the meanwhile, arranged for us.

My main purpose of going to Singapore was not for business. I had little interest in the venture. My main purpose was to see what had happened to my friends and how they were getting on.

Principally I was interested to see how Kwa Geok Choo and Milton Tan were getting on. They were my closest friends in College. Then there was also Chua Swee Sim whose family were family friends.

Milton was to become the President of the Automobile Association of Singapore and Kwa Geok Choo was to become a King's Scholar of Singapore and a well-known lawyer and the wife of the Prime Minister of Singapore, Lee Kuan Yew.

Even as I was about to set forth from the hotel, one of the workers of the hotel practically whispered to me to be careful and to take a trishaw if I could. The Japanese did not bother about the occupants in trishaws who were immediately obvious.

Was it that bad, I asked, taking the opportunity to find out something of the situation on the island. He told me of the massacre and of the comfort homes. He told me of some of the atrocities. He had not seen them, but he had heard. It was the same story of the war, the unnecessary and insensitive cruelty, the cold merciless immorality of the comfort homes, the callous attitudes of war and its inhumanity.

I then began to notice the gloom and the joylessness of the city. But for the presence of some furtive men the roads were empty. I had stepped from a hell to another hell.

Nevertheless I persisted even if I was later to regret it.

The first person I went to see was Milton. I had given no notice that I was coming and I really could not blame him for the welcome I received. Milton saw me outside his house. He did not even invite me in. There was a small garden outside his house, more like a widened passageway. He saw me at the end of this garden nearest to the road. His mother did not receive guests. There was no need to go to the house. I could see that I was not quite welcomed. Why, I did not know.

We stood outside the gate talking for an uncomfortable few minutes, it was a brief visit, it was plain that I should go soon. He could be considered a confidante, if not a best friend. I used to visit him in his home and he would let me use his car sometimes.

He told me of the death of Ebert who was not our favourite senior ragger in college. He was also a rugby scrumhalf and my rival who relegated me to the scrum because he was faster and had quicker reflexes. He was a volunteer and had been shot on Changi beach with the rest as a reprisal.

Other than that, he was out of touch with the others. He did not know what they were doing. That was the summing up of our conversation and it was about a death. I cannot remember if he said anything else. Such had been the effect of his experience of war and death.

I quickly ended my conversation and left. To think that I could have been so friendly with members of the enemy and yet become a stranger to one of my own. My reception was not what I had expected.

The next person I went to see was Geok Choo. We were contemporaries and she was also a friend of mine at college who commanded a great deal of respect for her intelligence, application and brilliance in her studies. I thought I would see how she was getting on.

She stayed in an apartment in the Tiong Bahru flats with her parents. It was not their habit to go out of doors and I thought I would drop in also on an unannounced visit.

She answered the doorbell and was obviously surprised to see me. How could I have come such a long way from Penang in such a situation. Was it safe to be outdoors? But, in answering that question I had an uneasy feeling about the flat and a sense of wonderment as to how I could have come from so far. I did not know why though she was kind enough to invite me into their kitchen since her father, she said, was occupying the living room.

There she offered me a cup of tea and explained that their sugar was rationed and scarce, but I could have some. I am not sure now if I refused the sugar or took a small spoonful. She was normally quiet and restrained and confident but, nevertheless, I could see something tragic had disturbed the household.

As I spoke I noticed that the several jars of sugar on the kitchen shelf from which she had taken her bottle, each had a label bearing the names of the individual members of the household. The father was systematic and had imposed a sort of control and order in the kitchen.

She also did not have much to tell me except that Kuan Yew was even then beginning, quietly at home, to prepare for his law after the war. As usual, he was single-minded, methodical, competitive and sharp as a razor.

There were some half-hearted attempts to carry on a conversation which fell rather flat. I wondered if that was either because there had been a tragedy in the family or the oppressive atmosphere, which pervaded Singapore, had reached the kitchen or both.

I think she was genuinely pleased to see me and to listen to news of mutual friends in Penang, yet I sensed that we seemed to be living within our own worlds. I left her after a while.

But the main purpose of my visit to Singapore had been fulfilled, if not on an enthusiastic note.

Since I still had time, I thought to look up Chua Swee Sim, also a college friend whose family were friends of the family. When they stayed in Penang, my mother and hers were on visiting terms and the children used to play in each others' homes. At least my mother would be happy to know how they were getting on. As old family friends I thought my welcome would be more open and less guarded.

She lived at the other end of town and it took a while to get there. When I finally arrived at the old mansion so familiar to me, I was confronted with a locked front door which took just as long as my ride there, for it to be opened. And then, I was confined to the porch.

When Swee Sim at last came to the door, it was only to tell me that her mother was not well and did not receive visitors. Since I was not invited in, I was left with the only presumption that included me who had come to visit the daughter apart from paying my respects to the mother. I am not sure if it was the effect of the war that had unsettled her mother. Whatever it was, this was my shortest visit that day.

On the journey back to my hotel, I fell to wondering if my visit to Singapore was worth all the effort that had been put into it.

As I reflected, it occurred to me that perhaps I had been too presumptuous. I had not given them prior notice of my visit. Turning up out of the blue suddenly, looking cheerful and confident, was perhaps not the best thing under the circumstances.

Few without special reason and, perhaps, special rights and a special purpose, would have travelled so far and with so apparent nonchalance. They had a right to be suspicious of me. They did not know what was happening in Penang and most normal people would have preferred to stay indoors and not go running round the peninsula in the face of a hostile enemy.

Fear and suspicion had made people cautious and circumspect. Informers abounded in Singapore and in Penang. I could not really blame anyone but the war and its aftermath.

That Milton who ought to have known me better than to suspect me was not, in a way strange. Survival was the keynote here and survival required keeping to oneself if possible. It was possible when I visited him he had kept communication with me as short as possible.

I realised that there was actually no point in dropping in on people in that climate of apprehension and mistrust. The war had made strangers out of friends, could it make strangers into friends?

It was time to return to the hotel. I never returned to Singapore again, till after the war. It was sad. I had become a stranger in Singapore. The war had turned friends into strangers.

But Singapore was not done with me yet. It was yet to surprise me.

Both surprises seem to have come from the fact that the Chinese-educated businessmen lived in their own cocoon, seemingly insulated from the war and the happenings of the other world.

Cho Suan's friends were in the hotel when I returned. There were discussions about the sale of our curry and if there was anything we wanted to take back to Penang. I wanted to take back medical items, which would be useful in a war, but fear of consequent suspicion that we might be terrorists by the *Kempeitai* was their advice against it.

So, that afternoon, we were asked to go to the office where the transaction was sealed with the promise that the money would be paid the next day. That done, we spent the rest of the afternoon talking of the possibility of future business.

I was to see another dimension of the world, the entirely strange new world with its own mores and independence of the Chinese businessman.

The discussions and the range of commodities offered showed a trade link and a network that stretched all the way from Bangkok to Singapore which seemed never to have been interrupted by the war but for the briefest of moments. There was still an almost completely intact and flourishing trade, though links with Europe had been completely severed by the war. The Chinese could survive on their own and would never starve to death.

Even as my English-speaking world was recovering from the initial shock of the war, filled with remorse and depression, confused, withdrawn, suspicious and afraid, unable to accept the unpalatable truth, somewhat filled with self-pity, in the seemingly impervious atmosphere of the cocoon, with little signs of self-pity, the Chinese business life had restarted and the Chinese traders were already reestablishing links with Thailand and a vigorous trade was quickly being rebuilt, matter of factly and despite the disruption of war.

Their network was extensive and the links stretched throughout Southeast Asia. Their system was intact because it was also intimate and no outsider could hope to penetrate it. It was clan orientated, established after hundreds of year of business. Thus it was the Teochews in the general trade whilst the Hokkiens dealt with some eighty per cent of the Chinese tea trade. Everybody knew everybody else in this circle.

Without my friend I would not have been able to do any trade. Had I come on my own, I might have lost my shirt in the matter of fact ruthlessness of the system. This was an eye opener. The Chinese need not have many friends outside their circle as long as this system existed. They are a viable people, a matter-of-fact race.

That night, the other surprise came. As we were waiting to be paid the next day, we were entertained to dinner. This was the custom, Cho Suan said, and I should attend even if I did not feel up to it. Again, another leaf of the life of the Chinese businessman was to unfold in front of me. I really did not have time for reflection and contemplation.

That night I was introduced to opium in which the fragile and innocent little 15-year-old girl was to play a part. I have recounted this episode earlier. Here my point is how the Chinese businessman could be so impervious as to the current thinking of the rest of the world on such matters. Was it because they read different newspapers and were aware of different things or was it that they were not bothered about others so long as they were not bothered by the others.

It was difficult to arrive at any sure conclusions and I thought to ask Cho Suan. He was, after all, subjected to the same things as I was. He did not think about it at all. His view was simple and direct. One directs one's mind to the facts. Questions of morality and ideology were of no concern to the businessman, his job was to conduct his trade and earn as much as possible. He was not responsible for the war, and fighting it was not his business. When there is fire, one calls the fire brigade, the rest stand by.

The Chinese business I knew was like that. They have a term for it and it was "practical". One has to be practical and each person has to solve his own problems and each one has his role, outside which he does not involve himself. If there is a war, let the soldiers do the fighting. They can pay for it.

Perhaps that is why the Chinese people survive but they cannot become great. For there can be no greatness if one is not a leader or our society does not possess great leaders.

And so, my episode in Singapore ended with the realisation that the Chinese will never throw stones because he does not have a cause. Things that do not directly concern him are no concern of his. He is practical and monetarily motivated.

I told Cho Suan the real reason why I had gone to Singapore. He looked surprised. Why could I not have had the patience to wait. It was fortunate that we had made a profitable trip, he said, and that we had not got into trouble. He would not have gone there for my reason. Was it worth it?

I thought for a long time in the train. Was it worth it for me? Was it *karma* that sent me to see friends who would have done just as well had I not gone there? In one trip, I had learnt a great deal, something I would never have done without the war. But was it chance or luck that I had gone through so much so far without hurting myself? Later events might provide the answer, but I don't know. Looking back though, I can only say that if my *karma* had not been good, or if chance had not provided me with so many good throws of the dice, I might not have survived the war. Perhaps someone could come up with an answer.

Cho Suan was to become a close business associate of mine, but he was only concerned with business and not interested in my thinking or my other activities. But it kept me practical. Though he was with me in Bangkok when we were bombed and we closely associated during the war, he never seemed concerned with the war. He is still alive but in retirement. He has survived and though, unknown, he is content and so he is happy. But he is still as unrelated to the rest of his society as he ever was. I suppose that if there is no striving, there can be no frustration. Without striving there can be little achievement, but, nevertheless, one is content and satisfied.

As we sometimes sit and watch
How the tiniest ripples can pervert
The truth by distorting the images
On the sea's surface, we also wonder
If we do not, by our emotions,
The truth distorts; provoking
The many grotesque faces of war.

23. THE TRUTH DISTORTS

AFTER receiving payment the next morning, we prepared for our empty journey back to Penang by the night train, the sadness of Singapore trailing behind. It was difficult to understand how war had affected the people so much. But then, I was beginning to understand that the nature of war is to compel change ruthlessly. It has to be so for change is not so easy to come by.

By the time we came to the end of our journey, the impending night curfew had stopped the ferry service for the day. There was nothing else but to pass the night at Prai station sleeping on the open platform part of which formed the apron of the station master's office, there being no accommodation anywhere nearby.

It would have to be an uncomfortable and a very cold night. The wind was whistling in from the sea, sweeping over the open platform persistently and unyieldingly. Despite my raincoat, I could not keep out the wind and the cold. Cho Suan did not have a raincoat. He suffered even more as such.

Just after midnight, we rose and shifted to the leeward side of the office which put us out of view of the actual platform for the arrival of the trains. This was not much better but at least we could get some sleep. But if we felt sorry for ourselves, it was nothing compared to what we were soon to see.

Early dawn the next day, cold and miserable, we were awakened by the screeching sound of the brakes. A train was pulling to a stop at the station. Then we heard guttural shouting in Japanese and the shuffling of boots on the cement floor of the platform which quickly brought us to our feet. We could not see what was going on as our view of the platform was obstructed by the office. But we felt that something was amiss and so we picked up our belongings to flee as we crept round the side of the office to have a better look.

It was about six thirty in the morning, time for the mail train to arrive from Singapore and Kuala Lumpur. But it was not the mail train but another train the engine of which was being detached from the train as we spied on the scene. The engine was being substituted by another for the train to continue northwards to Bangkok.

Standing on the platform in front of the standing train was a trainload of British prisoners of war, shuffling about in a ragged line and in front of them were some cauldrons of congee.

From the shoulder tabs of the young soldiers, they must have been from a battalion from the Cambridgeshire Regiment which formed part of the reinforcements that had landed in Singapore just in time to surrender to the Japanese. Their pink cheeks still with their apple rosy English bloom which I could see even in the gloom of the pre-dawn light as they shuffled and pushed to fall into line, made this obvious. They were awaiting further instructions.

Facing them were strutting soldiers in Japanese uniform who, I was told later, could only have been Korean guards who stood between them and the boiling cauldrons meant for the breakfast of the prisoners. For they were being taken to the ill-famed Death Railway.

Why they were allowed to land in Singapore when the Japanese were already storming into the city must have been an administrative error or it was a mystery. For there were no clear plans to put up a defence and, in the event, they did not even have a chance to fire their rifles before they were captured.

Soon their fresh bloom would disappear and their fresh full untanned skins and their youthful features would become sunken sallow bags and their new uniforms turned into rags.

They were innocent young kids who probably did not know what was going on, if they had been prepared for the rigours of war and the heat of the tropics. It was impossible to think that they could be the killers their duty required them to be. In any event, this was never put to the test. They never fired a shot. Nor would they ever, where they were going. Looking at them and the suntanned Japanese soldiers in comparison, one could not help feeling sorry for them.

Then, even as I watched, I saw something that hit me with a blow. The guard nearest to me lit a cigarette in front of the line, took a few puffs at it and then contemptuously spitting on it, deliberately threw it on the ground to crush it with his boot. He then took a few steps back and stood there arms akimbo as if he already knew what would happen.

What happened next was excruciatingly painful. It was a deliberate act, sadistic and humiliating. I would not have believed it if I had not seen it, especially as it was an act of a human done to another human being. But, no sooner had he stepped back to laugh at what would happen, as if he was practised, when two or three of the prisoners broke ranks and rushed forward to gather up the remains of the unburnt tobacco. Gathering it in their hands, they quickly began to roll the tobacco into a piece of paper into a smaller cigarette, lit it and immediately passed it round to a small group who had gathered around them to have a puff each.

The humiliation was unprovoked, it was sheer sadism; the guard knew what he was doing and what to expect and when they rushed forward for the cigarette, he started laughing loudly. I noted that though the other guards did not take part in all this, they seemed equally insensitive and unconcerned.

Nor did the other prisoners do anything. But they did not break ranks and kept to their line and so managed to maintain some dignity for the others. At least the guard had been unable to humiliate them.

As they kept to their positions and looked at those rushing forward for their smoke, there was a certain disdain and an aloofness which made the guard look a bit of a clown.

After a while, the guard, himself, lost interest and walked away and, upon a signal, the ranks were broken and the prisoners went forward eagerly for their meals ladled from the cauldron.

I shivered in the cold early morning wind. Unable to appreciate the humour of the guard and the insensitive nature of the other guards who had stood by, behaving as if nothing untoward was taking place. To them, it must have been a commonplace happening.

The ferry signalled its schedule for departure with its horn. We boarded it, in silence and soon we began to pitch and roll to the rising tide, I seemed to hear sighing and moaning as the ship strained and creaked at the seams. As the ship churned into the open sea of the channel, I idly looked over the bow. Thoughts about the war came to mind as I watched the clouds kaleidoscope in the waves and the sun sparkle in myriads of flashes as it was reflected by the waves.

I also smoked at that time and I hoped that the indulgent habit would not one day be my master. In fact, I determined, after what I had seen, that it would never be.

*Then, when the emotional winds die down
And our thoughts are stilled, we wonder
If we have not, to make grandiose our egos
And to satisfy the urges of our vanity,
Greed and ambition, used justice and beliefs
And religions as excuses to justify
The butchery of war and strife.*

24. URGES OF OUR VANITY

THE waters of the river Prai were still in the morning calm and the glassy surface reflected the almost undistorted reflections of the trees on the other side of the river. As we waited for the engine to start and the boat to cast off for the first of its many trips across the channel for the day, the tide began to turn and a gentle gust of the wind coming in from the sea, ruffled the surface of the water, breaking the images into a kaleidoscope of a myriad ever-changing images.

A quick shadow fell from an overhanging branch as a kingfisher took a dive at a minnow, breaking the surface of the water as it disappeared into the river to emerge with the fish which had itself been hunting for its food in the face of the rising tide; a predator with a prey.

The images on the surface of the river had been broken into meaningless fragments as the bird emerged with water spluttering from its heavily flapping wings and a trembling minnow held in its beak. It was life as it was also war.

I looked at the river with the shattered images and wondered how the kingfisher could have seen its prey and been so accurate in striking at a refracted image of the fish. I remembered how, as a young boy I had tried to spear at fishes only to strike at empty water.

Had nature built him that way that he might survive or was it that he was a kingfisher that he had adjusted himself to nature?

By the time the boat had turned round to head for the sea, the tide was beginning to run fast and a fresh breeze had helped to break up all fragments of the images into no more than little patches of light and shade. I gave up trying to see anything in the river any more.

Soon, the bow was slicing through the mouth of the river and the ferry, which was one of those which had taken the British officers to safety at the beginning of the war, began to rise and fall in the waves.

As the images broke and scattered in the wind, I wondered if one could say that the wind be metaphorically compared to our emotions which so disturb our calm as to distort the objective truths into such subjective ones so much so that what we see as truths are nothing more than perversions.

If we can say that, can we not then say further that the emotional storm of a war is of such violence that it would be impossible to see truths objectively and that our actions would be reactions only to mirages of the truth?

Our calm will be so disturbed that all we can see are no more than so many grotesque masks of war? Masks which we mistake for the many faces of war?

And there are so many ways of looking at them, of evaluating them, of interpreting or understanding them. Only that I was then too young to read any other meaning into them. A mirage was a mirage and an image was an image and that was that. I reacted to them as I saw them.

How should one view the war? Through the eyes of the Japanese or those of the British when both are fighting over colonies? Or should we view it from the eyes of the colonial subject? In each case, the ultimate answer would be different.

A Persian poem woven into a carpet says, "When any part of the body is sick, the whole body is in pain." But the pain suffered by the prisoners of war caused no pain to the Japanese. On the contrary, their feeling had been that of pleasure. But make no mistake about it. I am not taking sides. I think of those like the supposed Chinese villager who was supposed to have signalled the position of a British field headquarters in Ipoh who had been shot out of hand by his British captors. His pain did not cause pain either to those who shot him.

When Chandra Bose came and the Indian prisoners of war joined the Indian National Army, one thought them traitors. I did, anyway. But what if they had "liberated" India?

In our own acts of killing we feel righteous. Our propaganda deludes into believing that the cruel faces of war are those on the other side. The kind faces belong to us.

The fact is that we are all mirrors of our own soul and we all act according to our nature and according to our instincts for survival.

We fight for our own territory and we act in concert because we are social animals, encouraged by our propaganda. We protect each other and act in concert as an army purely out of social compulsion and necessity as social animals who must protect one another because we wish to survive.

We act as heroes only because we have to, often even by chance, not because we are the heroes we are made to believe we are.

We believe that our enemies are evil because, in that way, it is easier to inflict pain on them.

In the end, it is the war that is to blame. By its nature, war is an extreme measure of politics where the battlefield is the arena and the killing fields. To pretend that it comes because someone else is cruel and evil is trying to justify what cannot be justified.

The army is the national arm of war. Atrocities, or excesses, is one of the results and often personal. It is, nevertheless, an expression of war. To stop it, one has to stop wars.

We all have two sides, the good and the bad. Often, the same side looks different from both sides. It is always the enemy that sees the evil side. That refers to the front of the war. That is the front the enemy always see first.

But, behind it, behind the battle lines, there is the amorphous mass where we begin to see the individual faces, the individual face behind the national face of the propaganda posters. They present the confused and conflicting images of the man in the street. They are the innocent victims on both sides, caught in the webs of war.

Yamagata and Kirita, the nurses, were of such from the other side. I was still to see other faces as the war unfolded.

Then I watched another jellyfish twisting and turning in the waves and my mind drifted back to see the sadistic delight I saw in the face of the guard at Prai station.

Many of us could have been like that little man strutting about his puny stage just as my insurance agent turned detective officer was who loved to see the rich crawl to him.

"Call me sir."

I could hear his voice above the sound of the waves swishing by the bow of the ferry. Then I heard him continue and asked that the word "sir" be repeated in a louder tone.

"Louder." His imagined voice came through the sound of the wind. Brave words for a man already in a dream of greatness. We could have been like him too, friend or foe.

The meaning of war may vary with the individual and the nationality. The images are as variable as the images reflected by the surface of the uncalm sea. There is no objective truth in the mirages which depend on who is looking at the sea.

But the real truth is the same, only that we cannot find it because we are subjectively made.

Perhaps, in the calmest of ways when you can look below the surface, you might see another reality below. On the surface, you can see another level below where another reality lurks. But then, there is yet another level below that where the largest creatures live.

That is also the layer of the subconscious where the primeval truths lie which defies logic and the reasoning which defines our actions but which yet do influence them.

Is that the truth then? The truth which sees us as puny corpuscles in the organism of the universe playing our puny little parts as our corpuscles play their little parts within us.

Are the reasons for war and peace to be found there and that for all our reasoning and philosophies, we are acting to the dictates of a higher order like the way the frogs and the ants fight their wars by instinct, for all our argument that we are of a higher order of animals who can look at the stars and talk in abstract terms of heaven and of religious and spiritual things.

In the history of the world, tribes have fought tribes, states have fought states, nations have fought nations and each time the conflict grows bigger and bigger and the world shrinks smaller and smaller. Today, wars are fought between combinations of nations and one day the war will be large enough for the overcrowded and dirtied world to cleanse and end itself.

And all this because that is written in heaven and the *karma* of the world which puts it out of our power and reasoning?

I suppose, only the Eye knows.

Can I also suppose that like the sun that gives us life and the moon that gives us our romances, so also the unknown forces within us will lead us from war to war until we lose all?

Such are the universal truths that only the Eye can know but it can only beam at us benevolently, for it cannot speak.

The ship's bells rang, the engine stopped and the boat slowly came to a stop. I had arrived back at the island. The interlude, the nightmare at Prai, had come to an end. But the carbuncle of war was yet to rid itself of all its poisons and subside.

I was to return to yet another such carbuncle whose poison might have resulted in the people of Penang becoming a society of gamblers.

Soon after things had settled down and the comfort homes were established, the Japanese took over one of the parks (the New World Park at Swatow Lane, to be precise), and turned it into a gaming park where gambling stalls were set up and where the people were encouraged to gamble away whatever they still had.

It was supposed to have been established by the mistress of Suzuki, the Penang *Kempeitai* chief, in conjunction with her friends and with his encouragement.

The most famous of these games was *Tai Sai* (or, literally, Big or Small). I did not play the game and do not know all the variations of the modes of the game. But, in general, the game consisted of a card of diagrams where the players could stake on 'Big' or 'Small' or odds on colours and so on with different odds.

In front of the operator was a dish with an upturned bowl under which were two ordinary dice. After the gamblers had placed their bets on appropriate squares on the diagram in front of them, the operator would lift the bowl to expose the dice. Since each dice has six faces numbered one to six, those who had staked on 'Big' would win if the two uppermost faces of the two die amounted to more than six and those who had staked on 'Small' would lose. Should the total of these two dice amount to exactly six, the operator would be the winner except for those who had staked on six.

Penang was not known for its gambling before the war. But it became well known for its gamblers after that. My mother, who was no gambler, began to frequent the place. Though she was not a big player, I used to go there to keep an eye on things. But many were not so controlled and it was there when I was offered a daughter for a week by a father for a carton of cigarettes.

Such lessons were salutary. Why the Japanese encouraged gambling I do not know. But it was sad to see so many people flocking to the park night after night throughout the war and exposing their weakness of character, and the ruthless way it was exploited. This weakness for gambling which became a sound weakness to be caught up in the gambling habit in such as the hundred-character game which swept through the country after the war.

God works in mysterious ways.
Even as the end draws near
And our breasts begin to swell
With hope and the insanity,
The nightmares and the dreams
Draw to a close, all we can see is
Blood on the golden sands.

25. GOD WORKS IN MYSTERIOUS WAYS

SEET was a Taiwanese who had come to the island as a police interpreter with the Japanese government. He lived up the road and soon befriended my father whom he came genuinely to admire to such an extent that he adopted himself and came to look upon my father as his, even calling upon him to officiate his marriage to a daughter of his landlord.

He was a small man, a frequent visitor to the house when the gold tooth in his mouth would give a ray of golden sunshine to and whose voice would ring through the house.

Seet had a warm and open manner, a bright open face and an easy smile which could win over many suspicious hearts. But a day came which would change all that and send a chill into the relationship he had established with us even if it was not entirely his doing.

Towards the end of the war, a marauding British submarine, probably the same one that had fired the shot that sank the junk in which my friend, the sundry shopkeeper with the 16-year-old wife and son, killing my friend, sending my friend's wife into prostitution, was to come across two Japanese cargo boats leaving Penang in the early morning tide to sink them both.

The first vessel was sunk just after the Muka Head lighthouse and the second was caught off Pulau Kendy.

It was the biggest blow Japan ever suffered in the vicinity. The ships were fully laden and had set sail before dawn in the utmost secrecy even if probably at near high tide as the channel of Penang harbour was a shallow one.

Though the sinking was probably a lucky chance, they at first suspected that it came as a result of information transmitted from the island itself.

This sinking had taken place at the back of the island and within sight of inshore fishing boats and when they returned to the island, news began to spread round the island like wildfire.

Seet was an inquisitive man with a talkative nature and it was this that got him into trouble with the *Kempeitai*. He was not made of sterner stuff. He had heard the news in a coffeeshop that morning and had excitedly spread the news of the sinking.

The Japanese *Kempeitai* had also heard of the sinking and was anxious to know how the submarine came to know of the sailing times of the ships. When they heard the news from the public of the sinking, they began to trace the origin of the news and they finally traced it to Seet.

Thinking that he must have been involved with someone who was in communication with the British as the news was traced to him, he was immediately arrested and tortured, regardless of the fact that he had so faithfully worked for the Japanese for so many years.

According to Seet, they beat him again and again. Then they gave him the water treatment. Finally, they suspended him from a beam with his hands which were tied behind his back till they slowly rose to end above his head. The pain was immense and he collapsed finally.

Seet was a devoted character as was witnessed by the way he cared for his wife till she died in Malacca where they went after the war but he was not made of sterner stuff.

Perhaps it is wrong of me to say that, for it is doubtful if anyone tortured the way he was could have held back anything for long.

So he "confessed". He had but a friend he could think of in Penang. It was us. So he said that the news had come from my brother. But how did my brother get hold of the news? He knew we had Claremont up the hill with its estate. Where then could we have kept the radio? Obviously up the hill at Claremont.

The *Kempeitai* was not so much interested as to how the news of the sinking was discovered as to how news of the ships' schedule was known to the submarine which had caught the ships as they left the harbour. Someone must have sent a radio signal to the enemy and they wanted to know who did it. It had to be someone who had a clear view of the harbour and our house up the hill had such a clear view.

So they came to our house the next morning and took my father and my brother into custody.

The truth was that there was no such radio nor was my brother in any way responsible. Seet had heard the news when he was having coffee early that morning and he had overheard an excited fisherman who was out at sea that night and was returning to base at the Bayan Lepas when the explosion and sinking had caught his attention.

Seet, who could not keep his mouth shut over such exciting news had begun to broadcast it to his friends and an informer had heard it.

Nor was anyone responsible for sending out any message. A few days later, the news of the sinking was broadcast over the air by the BBC that a British submarine on routine patrol which was having a last look round the area of the entrance of the North channel of Penang had caught sight of the two cargo ships as they left port.

No one had given them any advance information, it was a chance encounter on a routine patrol and the submarine had maneuvered itself to sink one of the ships just outside the channel before it turned its attention on the other ship to stalk and sink it off Pulau Kendy almost within sight of the shore where fishermen saw the flash of the explosion and the sound of the torpedo which had struck the ship squarely.

Both the ships had been sunk. But, until the submarine returned to base, no one knew the truth and Penang was abuzz like a hornet's nest that had been struck by a sling shot and Seet, my father and my brother had suffered as a consequence.

I was not in the house but as soon as I heard the news I went there through the back of the house which opened to Chow Thye Road behind. We were surprised that the *Kempeitai* had just arrested the man they had put in the highest civilian post as the high court judge.

Fate decided that Susumu was to fly into Singapore that morning from Burma, obviously on a military mission. Chance had it that a local man should also have gone to Singapore that morning who had heard the news of my father's arrest.

The two met by chance and Susumu asked if the man knew the family of my father. He did indeed and he told Susumu that before he left the island that very morning, he had heard that my father and a son had been arrested by the *Kempeitai*.

On hearing this, Susumu lost no time hitching a ride to Penang and was able to board a plane to Penang. He had then gone to the *Kempeitai* and had managed to pledge himself in writing as guarantor for our integrity, thus putting his life at risk. That done, he had at once returned to Singapore by the same plane as he had to return the next day to Burma. Again, he had happened to be around when we needed him.

That evening they released my father who came running home, probably to take his usual exercise as well as in elation. He had not been touched whilst in detention.

My brother was released two days later. He was able to tell us that he had been confronted with Seet who had immediately pleaded for forgiveness, saying that he had been forced to say what was not true. Of course, my brother was indignant that he had been implicated as he had not been to the hill since the time we returned from it after the evacuation.

According to my brother, he had simply called Seet a liar nor did we have any radio which, in any event, would not have been capable of transmitting any news.

According to him, apparently the *Kempeitai* officer who brought in Seet to confront him, knew sufficient English to understand what was said and so he was not touched as well and he was released the next day.

According to Seet, who was himself released about a week later, when news from the BBC was announced and the truth was known he was also released upon which he immediately came to the house to beg for forgiveness from my father on his knees. That was Seet.

Of all the versions, the most bizarre was that of Susumu. We did not know of his version till he came to see me one evening after our dinner and for want of somewhere better to go, I went with him to Gurney Drive where we sat on the sea wall and listened to the waves lapping the shore.

It was strange to hear how he had chanced to be sent to Singapore and there to have met a local by chance who had also that very morning of the arrests arrived in Singapore who knew our family and the news of the arrests.

That he was able to hitch a plane ride to Penang by a plane going to Penang and back that same morning was also almost a near impossibility.

Soon after he had met me this last time in the war, rumours of the Imphal invasion attempt percolated through the grape vine. When the news came through of its failure, I wondered if he had been caught in the fighting and if he had survived. My mind went back to that last night at Gurney Drive.

It was a dark night and the tide was rising. As we sat and he told me how he had happened to be in Penang, there was a certain amount of incredulity in me. Not because I did not trust him but how it ever could have happened that so many times the dice of fate had rolled in my favour.

As he narrated the events from his point of view, I gathered that he had not even bothered to find out if I or my brother had been arrested. What he assumed I do not know to this day as I did not think it important. It was the fact that he had come forward to guarantee us without hesitation that was the important thing.

He had done a dangerous thing few would have undertaken and he had done it for one from the occupied territory. That he thought his guarantee was important showed his confidence in himself. Besides, he had nothing to gain.

Then, as we watched the tide, I suddenly asked him quietly, "What would you do if we were both drowning and there was only one plank between us?"

"I would push the plank towards you and swim away," came the unhesitating reply.

My question was spontaneous. It came out of the blue. His answer was equally spontaneous. That was enough.

We had parted that night and he returned to the front. Now had come rumours that at Imphal the Indian soldiers sent there had also deserted to return to India.

Then I wondered if he had come that night because he did not know what would happen to him.

I hoped he would write after the war and let me know if he was safe but he did not. When I returned to Penang after my studies in England I wrote to his university and was given an address in Mitsubishi. I wrote to him, but the letter did not reach him.

I found him again some twenty years later after the memories of the war had faded. By then he had become the Managing Director of Mitsubishi Trading and was soon to become one of the 26 chairmen of the Mitsubishi group before his retirement.

I have not seen him since.

Where the golden grass will grow
The red poppies will also grow.
From the mud comes the lotus,
With deaths come new births.

Even when deep hatred runs the heart,
Love does not really die but hides
In the deep warmth of the soul to return,
Like the faithful golden orioles in spring.

26. LIKE THE GOLDEN ORIOLES IN SPRING

WITH Susumu Ogawa came the most touching friendship I ever encountered. He was only two years older than I was and, ironically, a Japanese staff officer, one of those who would have planned the military campaign in Malaya if he had not been a staff officer in the Burma command. War cannot be like a chessboard for then he would have been on the other side. Yet he was a soldier though he could never have been my enemy. He also wore a mask of war which did not befit his sensitive soul.

Susumu, though he was a Japanese officer, became my best friend during the war if not the best friend I ever had. He was more than a friend. He saved my life, not once but twice.

There is no more apt description about this sort of relationship than the Chinese one which is that of a *kooi jin*.

A *kooi jin* is even more than a wife. It is someone from a past life who has come to repay you a debt or to help you or save you from a misfortune for no apparent reason at all. He is a spiritual friend who will come in your hour of need and leave you after he has done what is necessary.

That was what he was to me. What I was to him is best put in his own words. I lost touch with him after the war for some twenty years. When I found him again he was already the Managing Director of Mitsubishi Trading in Tokyo after the war and he was about to become one of the twenty-six prestigious chairmen of the Mitsubishi group.

We met in Tokyo and he still could not speak English so he had an interpreter with him. He was writing his memoirs, he told me. But he would not be mentioning me and he hoped I would understand it. For it was Japanese custom, he explained, not to write about the most personal and intimate relationships and things. It was not good form.

There was no reason to doubt his words. He need not even have told me he was writing his memoirs. After all, it would be in Japanese and I would not understand it. In any event he would not lie in the presence of an interpreter who was also one of the officers of Mitsubishi.

I suppose I did. To me it was the same. I do not subscribe to "keyhole" writings either, especially sexual affairs which would make good but vulgar reading, unless, of course, when it is necessary to explain a certain point.

I was flattered by that sentiment, translated to me by his interpreter. Coming in 1976, after we had lost contact with each other for so many years, it was the best credential of a friendship ever made.

But we have no such tradition as the Japanese had. In fact, public acknowledgment of a gratitude to a friend is not bad form at all. It is common in English literature and I thought I would disagree with him when the time came. The time has come I will have to narrate our friendship for it was one of the faces of war which, perhaps, should never be ignored or forgotten.

Call it *karma*, or fate, or what you will, for our meeting was in the odds of a million to one.

I had decided to take a short stay of two weeks at Claremont, taking the train down every morning to go to work when, one afternoon, just on the last week of my stay, I saw a young Japanese officer with a blue ribbon on his sword, occupying a compartment waiting for the train to start.

I knew, from the colour of the ribbon that he could only be a lieutenant in the army.

Hoping to avoid him, I took the next compartment and then got off when I arrived at Claremont station whilst he continued his journey up the hill.

This went on for a couple of days or so. Whenever I came to the station to board my train, he would be there, sitting by himself in a compartment waiting for the train to start; and on seeing him, I would take the other compartment so that we would both sit in splendid isolation.

Then, one afternoon, when the train stopped at Claremont and the conductor of the train came to open the door of my compartment for me to alight, I saw him signalling to the conductor to open the door of his compartment as well.

It was clear that he wanted to follow me out of the train but the reason for this was unclear to me. Yet, there could be no other ostensible reason why he was getting out of the train unless he wanted to see where I was going.

He looked a decent serious young man, more in the line of a scholar than a fighting man. But he was a Japanese officer and I must admit that his alighting at the station caused some fear in me.

My fears grew when I noticed him standing at the station and observing me as I set off to my home. There were rumours that there were some anti-Japanese elements hiding up the hill and though they kept a very low profile and did not cause any harm, I was afraid that he might be following me because of his suspicions. One did not expect to meet friendly enemy officers and I did not know why he was up the hill.

I took my time as I left the station to see if he would be following me. But he did not. He merely stood at the station as if he was wondering what he should do. But I felt he would follow me.

I happened to have been up there. But my honeymoon, having married my wife in what can only be said to be another aberration of war. For we married because of a need for "good form" because we had our future and studies mapped out by the war and the war had forced upon us each other. She was in Claremont and we were not ready for marriage. That was a threat upon us. I was buccaneer in spirit, she was young, homely and looking for security.

On reaching home I prepared my wife, it was a wartime marriage, for the worst. I told her to keep out of sight and asked her to take the back path down to the middle station if anything should happen to me.

A few minutes later, the dogs barked from the path leading past the caretaker's bungalow from the station to the house. I knew who it must be. I put on my shoes and went round the side of the house to the back and there, standing beside the swimming pool immediately behind the building, was this young Japanese officer.

Then a welcome and surprising thing happened. This young Japanese officer, on seeing me, took off his cap, he was shaven in the manner of all Japanese soldiers, and took a deep bow.

It was surprising because I did not expect any Japanese to bow to us. It was welcome because to them it was good manners and a mark of respect. The anxiety in me faded. No hostile Japanese officer would bow to any of his intended victims. It was becoming clear that by his bow he had intended to put me at my ease. I quickly returned the bow.

Then, another surprise came. In halting English, he asked if he could come into the house. I took him round to the front steps of the house and when he was about to go up the steps, he began to take off his boots.

It is customary for one to take off one's shoes when entering a house. But it was difficult for him to take off his boots. It was not necessary for him to do that if we were only going to sit in the front of the house. Besides, I was not sure if it would do for me to let him do what he was trying to do without some form of protest.

But he insisted and I let it go. He took off his boots and came up the steps into the hall and we sat at the table in the centre of the room. By now I was already more at ease.

Then he told me who he was and what he was doing up the hill. He was a staff officer from Burma. He had been sent to Penang to recuperate up the hill for a few weeks because the doctors had discovered a shadow in his lung. Something had been taken from him which had been sent to Japan and they were waiting for the results and that as soon as he was pronounced fit, he would be returning to service.

He had seen me on the train and thought he would acquaint himself with me. Why, he did not say, but at least I now knew that he had not been motivated by suspicions which was a good thing.

His English was halting and it was clear he was not used to speaking it at all. But the strange thing was that we seemed to be able to communicate with each other more through telepathy than anything else and became familiar with each other even before the evening was out and he had to return to the train before the sun was down and to the top of the hill where he was staying.

After introducing himself, he began to take stock of what was in the room. His eyes fell on the few volumes of *Halsbury's Laws of England* standing in the book cases at both ends of the hall which ran the whole front of the bungalow. That seemed to settle his mind as to who we were.

He asked if I was a lawyer. I told him my father was but I was not. He said he was qualified as a magistrate at the Tokyo Imperial University. It seemed that in Japan, the brightest students could choose to go on to pass the magistrate's exams which were of a higher level.

He wondered why I was up in the hills. He thought, when he first saw me, that I was a kind of poet or philosopher. According to the best Japanese traditions, the solace and quietude of the hills were meant for sages and those were the more elderly and he had wondered why someone as young as myself should be up there. It was this that had intrigued him as he decided to follow me to the house.

It was flattering but I was no sage nor did we have this tradition in Penang. Nor was I studying law.

I liked what I saw in front of me. He had a quiet demeanour, a serious smile and a slightly hawkish nose and appeared not to have a frivolous sense of humour but our seemingly impossible, strange and somewhat mystic friendship had begun.

Susumu did not agree with the war. He made it quite plain right from the very beginning. He had no business to be in uniform, he was not a volunteer but a conscript.

Our house has a nice open view of to the city which was then glowing in the evening sun. He looked at the scene and commented on how nice the view was. He thought that it had an ideal atmosphere for a writer. One could write poetry here, he observed.

To me, that first meeting was enough of an introduction to him. I was interested and wrote poems and his culture and breeding and his affinity with me must have caused him to sense this affinity between us.

It was as if kindred souls had met. Even as our friendship was being sealed, dusk was falling and he took his leave.

Had he not had a shadow in his lung and if we did not have Penang Hill, he would never have gone there. Had my wife not been coerced by her grandmother to marry me to keep good form with the neighbours since I was staying with them as the only male person then, I would not have been up the hill and we would never have met.

As it was, both of us were on the hill for two weeks and that we should have met in that brief two weeks of uncoordinated stays was nothing short of a miracle.

From the first moments one could sense a strange sense of bondage between us and when it was time for him to go, I saw him off at the station.

I did not expect to see him again till we next met on the train, if he happened to use the same train, and I would be leaving the hill within the next few days.

But early the next morning, I heard the dogs barking again. I went round to the back of the house and he was coming up the path to invite me for a breakfast with him at Crag Hotel, where he was the sole occupant.

I did so and at breakfast he informed me he had to have breakfast with me. He had a phone call the night before to tell him that the results of his medical tests had come and he had to go down the hill for the results and further tests and, if they were negative, he would not be returning to the hill again.

The breakfast was because of the news and he was afraid he might not see me again. I reciprocated by telling him that I would also be leaving the hill before the weekend.

He asked me for my city address. He was not sure if he would be leaving at once or if there had to be more tests or even if he might not come up the hill again. If he could do so, could he visit me?

Again, I thought, I would not see him again. Our paths had crossed only for the briefest of moments but there was no good reason why they should cross again and again.

The breakfast was so Chinese with congee in a bowl, a few bits of salted fish, pickled olives, a salted hard-boiled egg and a cup of Japanese tea, that I briefly wondered if he had ordered it specially for me. But then, it could also be Japanese. How close were both our cultures, I thought.

We both came down the hill by the same train. I dropped off at Claremont and he went on down the hill. That would be the last, I thought.

He came the next weekend and I introduced him to my father and mother and asked him to stay for dinner. He did so and the next week he came again.

The next day, I began to feel uncomfortable and a fever soon developed which put me to bed. No one knew what it was. When our local doctor came, he was not sure either. We had to wait. Without laboratories and clinical tests, no one could be sure and the only laboratory Penang had in the General Hospital was not available to us.

One of my cousins had only died a year or two before of the same illness and no one knew the identity of the disease and we knew that even if it was typhoid, which came at that time of the year every year during the season of rambutans, there was no other treatment but fluids and to ride out the illness on his own energy and reserves, since typhoid caused eruptions on the linings and stomach which solid food could lacerate, leading to perforations, bleeding and painful death.

The illness takes fourteen days to reach its crisis level before it works itself out by that time most would have succumbed through lack of food and resistance. So I was put to bed and given fluids as the fever slowly mounted.

Susumu turned up that Sunday to find me in that condition and with a slowly mounting fever. But delirium had not come. I could see him but I could hardly speak to him.

He went off and later returned with a Japanese doctor, looking equally young. The doctor examined me, repeating all the while that he was not supposed to look after civilians because he was a military doctor and that we were not to tell anyone about him. He had come because Susumu was his college friend.

It was a remarkable coincidence that he should have met up with Susumu, an accident which probably saved my life.

I could see that he was nervous and the fact that we were not only civilians but locals was putting him into double jeopardy. He then went off because he could do little else on a Sunday. But the next morning he returned, by then I was worse. I cannot remember if he had done any other examination or taken any specimen.

But he came to confirm that I was suffering from typhoid fever and I should be kept in isolation. Before he left he handed over some pills which, he said, would keep up my strength to fight the illness. I think what he gave me were some sort of vitamin pills. I was to take no food.

At the mention of pills, my mind woke up. I remembered that I had a stock of MB693 pills which I had hidden away for such emergencies. I asked that I be given a course of those pills, thinking that if the illness was due to bacteria, they could at least fight them.

Then I faded away and slowly, I was told, I went into a delirium which went on and on till the fourteenth day.

That day fell on a Sunday. Susumu apparently came that day to spend the night in the house. The next morning he said goodbye to the family saying that he would be leaving Penang and that was the last time they ever saw him again.

I did not know all this. I was in delirium. I woke up one afternoon thinking of rambutans because I knew that the typhoid season was also rambutan season. I was not aware I had awakened from a delirium. In fact, I did not know I had even gone into a delirium. It was when I had recovered enough to enquire about him that I was told what happened on the night of the crisis.

Susumu, it seems, came almost every day to see how I was getting on. One night, he stayed back for the night. He told my mother that he had received permission to be away from his barracks for the night. He stayed for dinner with the family.

Towards the end of the dinner, he suddenly thought to explain why he was there that night, in case the family did not know, by announcing loudly to everyone at the table that it was the fourteenth day of my illness and that it was my crisis night. If I pulled through that night, he continued, I would be on my way to recovery.

My brother tried to dismiss his fears by assuring him that he was sure nothing would happen and that there was nothing to worry about. But Susumu did not have that sense of humour. He did not think that I should have been dismissed so casually, such an attitude was not to be found in Japanese culture.

To everyone's surprise, he rose in his chair and looking across the table at my brother, exclaimed in disbelief, "Your brother may be dying and you joke like that."

He sat down, refused to continue with his dinner and waited for everyone to finish. There was silence at the table and a great deal of pretence at eating.

No amount of placating would have made him continue his dinner. Then, asking to be excused as soon as everyone had finished eating, he came upstairs to my room insisting that he sleep there.

As typhoid is contagious my mother would not take the risk and he was forced to sleep in the room next door.

Apparently he did not sleep very well that night and came to my room frequently. Early the next morning he was up and dressed to go back to the barracks.

That afternoon, Susumu came to tell my mother that he had come to say goodbye. He had received instructions to return and he would be leaving Penang for good and that he would be leaving to rejoin his unit at the war front. Our friendship had hardly lasted a month. When I woke up that afternoon after the crisis had passed, with my first thoughts I turned my head on my pillow to look for the rambutans out of the back window against which my bed had been placed.

But all I saw were the black and white of the roadside trees outside the window towards the West. I could not see rambutans nor any colour but black and white.

Strange, I thought, when one is too sick, one can only see silhouettes and nothing more than a white sky and black twigs. Colour was something not immediately observable. But I could see it was in the afternoon.

Then I fell asleep. The next time I was conscious again, I had become more alert. It was morning. I could see sunlight playing on the leaves and the trunk of a tree outside the eastern window.

I could even hear the oriole calling outside the window. I looked out and saw the yellow bird with a pinkish bill and black wings flying towards the trunk of the tree and picking up a lizard and then flying away.

Strange, I can now see colour and hear birds singing. Then I fell asleep again.

A few nights later, I was awakened by sounds of my father and mother in the breakfast room below my room. There was no one in my room. The insistence of the argument forced me out of bed. I stood up shakily and saw my figure reflected from the cupboard mirror for the first time after my illness. I was astonished to see how thin and gaunt I was. But it was not how ill I had been that struck me when I saw that image but how similar to Abraham Lincoln I looked with my hair. It was the only thing that told me how long I had been ill.

I slowly moved across the room to the door, I did not yet know how long my illness had been and how weak I had become till I staggered and nearly fell. Then, through the upstairs hall, down the stairs, the front hall and the dining hall to the breakfast room I went.

No one had seen me go all this way and even as I entered the breakfast room where they were still arguing they were not aware of my presence.

I called out to them. Why were they quarrelling even as one of their children was dying, I asked. I spoke loudly, but I am not sure if I was strong enough to have spoken above a whisper.

They stopped arguing and looked up as if they had seen a ghost. Then both came rushing towards me to hold me up and to take me back to my room. I am not sure if I did save a marriage that night.

As soon as I had recovered sufficiently, my thoughts turned to Susumu. How was I to view the presence of the oriole that had called out to me. Immortalised by a Tang poem, one of the three hundred poems translated by Arthur Waley, as a symbol of eternal love, the golden oriole is paired for life and returns in spring year after year after flying ten thousand miles to the South for the winter to renew their love amidst the spring blossoms with the faithful fire of the eternal love burning for ever in their breasts.

And I wondered if it was the spirit of Susumu, returning from faraway Burma to see how I was getting on and to wish me good morning.

Now, sound the trumpets,
Let the bugles blow,
Cover those faces now at peace
Bury the coffins, then,
Instead of salutes, let them
Dig trenches, plant roses,
Grace the ponds with lotus flowers.

27. SOUND THE TRUMPETS

ONE day in early 1945, something of great significance happened. I vaguely recall it as being in February when Yamagata excitedly asked me at an Eposho meeting if I was interested to purchase dried rice from Bangkok if he could arrange for an import permit.

Rice was a rationed item and its movements were entirely controlled by the authorities. But the Chinese merchants had thought of the idea to briefly cook rice and then drying it to be sold as cooked rice. This took it out as a rationed item, so, even if it remained a controlled item, as was the case with all food commodities, it was no longer a rationed item and could be dealt with provided it could be imported and permits for its movements were applied for.

What was surprising was not the prospect of importing the rice, it was that the Japanese were now formally ready and willing to help us import rice. The fact that he was to get a permit for it was exciting as it meant that there had been a relaxation of the export of such an important item as rice; and this led to many resulting speculations.

It could mean that Thailand was now producing more rice, which was a slim possibility; or that Japan did not now need to import so much, again a slim possibility; or that the blockade of Japan was beginning to tell, which was a greater possibility.

I pondered over the implication of this offer for a while. Perhaps the Japanese wanted to know the system used by the rice millers of Thailand to sell their rice. After all, the best way to know any operation is to join the gang. After all, the rice trade was run by Teochews and we already know that they did not welcome strangers into their system.

Then the most interesting thought of all came over me. Was this a sign that the war was coming to an end? It was a dangerous but the most exciting impression of all.

Finally I approached Cho Suan with the proposition, taking care not to mention the impression that had been uppermost in my mind. Nor did he ask me what I thought. But he jumped at the offer. It was too good to miss, he said.

He was not even inquisitive as to who Yamagata was. He did not even want to know why Yamagata was being so helpful. In a way, I suppose the Chinese are like that. So long as a proposal was practical and suited them and there was nothing apparently suspicious, it was enough.

Most of the rice mills of Thailand were situated along the mighty Mekong River which flowed from the rice fields into and through Bangkok into the Gulf of Thailand. If Yamagata could get us the permit, it meant a safe travel to and from Thailand with rice, something which made the risk worthwhile.

Finally, we found ourselves on a train to Bangkok. The understanding was that there would be no strings attached. Yamagata would come along with us to guarantee our safe passage and we would buy all the rice we could transport out of Bangkok and sell it as a controlled item ourselves without having to give any to anyone else.

We arrived in Bangkok after an uneventful journey. Even the clearance at the border of Malaya and Thailand was uneventful. Yamagata was our passport and our protection against the Japanese officer who came through the train just before we reached the border.

As soon as we got into Bangkok and had put ourselves into a hotel, Cho Suan went to work. He took us directly to the rice mill of "Thye Hin Chan" on the bank of the mighty Mekong River in down town Bangkok. Bingo, it was a strike on the first throw. There was rice everywhere in the mill, some of which was clearly ready for sale.

The owner was a Teochew, a man in his forties, fat and contented. He was not short of rice. The office and the mill adjoined the drying yard. There we saw mountains of rice piled in heaps beside some huge pots of boiling water and rice drying in the open yard. The smell of rice cooking filled the air and steam rose from the pots.

For a while we watched the workers pouring rice into the pots, stirring the pots and then quickly ladling the rice out again, making sure that only the skin of the rice was cooked, so as not to spoil its flavour, but cooked enough not to be taken as rice which was rationed.

We watched them making use of the scorching sun and the cement floor of the yard to heat and dry out the rice. It saved paying for energy that way. This was the rice we had come for.

Either the harvest that year had been spectacular or there must have been a bottleneck in the delivery system somewhere. Even if we were starving in Malaya, rice was overflowing the warehouses of the mill. Rice was piled heap upon heap, and every heap almost a mountain and running even into the mighty Mekong.

The mill was full of rice in every stage of their production process. Rice being readied for cooking, cooked rice drying in the sun, dried rice shovelled into heaps being poured into bags, rice in bags piled near the entrance of the yard ready for loading into transport, rice in the warehouses and godowns. Something must be wrong.

We went into the office. When tea was poured out, Chinese style, it was obvious that there was little difference in his culture and that of his counterpart in Penang or Singapore. He lived much as the overseas Chinese or British expatriates lived out in the tropics, in his own style and almost immune to the culture of Thailand, thinking of a home he would not return to in China.

He poured us out some Chinese tea as we sat round his table to negotiate. His godowns were overflowing and he could give us immediate delivery. Immediate was not soon enough. We wanted delivery before the train left for Malaya the next day and he was only too willing to oblige because he had no space left for the rice waiting for him up river.

There was no problem. As with his counterpart in Singapore who had received our chicken curry, he would do everything necessary for us, arrange for the wagon and the delivery, see that everything was loaded and all we had to do was to pay him before we left.

All our business done, he invited us to the normal dinner that night as purchasers such as us were wont to expect as we left the premises.

That was fine. We had been registered in a hotel in downtown Bangkok, quite close to his yard to make it convenient for everyone. We would be ready to roll the next day after spending only a night in Bangkok.

We took our leave, went off to unpack and thought of taking a look at Bangkok, but changed our minds as looking around aimlessly was not worthwhile under the circumstances. Finally, we had a wash and rest and prepared ourselves for dinner.

Yamagata was present at the dinner so it was quite a formal uninformative one. No one discussed the war in Thailand which was what we most wanted to do. But the bits of conversation we had over dinner was such as to give us a good patchwork view of the war.

Business was not too good. His business was not too good either. He had too much rice because the harvest had been good but no one was buying. Thailand was an exporter of rice. So was Burma, its neighbour. So business was bad and no one was buying meant Japan wasn't buying. The rest of the conclusions we had to draw for ourselves.

There were rumours from Burma. People there were also finding things difficult and they were restless and unhappy. That could only mean that the Japanese were not advancing into India as planned.

The rest of the world news we already knew. Japan had depended on Germany for the depletion of western forces in Asia. If Germany lost the war, could Japan be far behind? Nothing could prevent us from knowing that the Allied forces had beaten back Germany from the African continent and her armies were folding up in Italy and Europe was on the point of liberation and the net was closing in on Japan in the Pacific.

Our speculation was being confirmed in Bangkok. The blockade of Japan was beginning to tell. Her sea lanes were being throttled. She was under siege? But discretion required us to keep our remarks short. Everyone at the table knew what the others were thinking.

As if in confirmation of our suspicions, after we had gone to bed, the planes came that night. I made a mental note of the date and if I am not wrong it was on the night of February 14 that I saw a lone B29 caught in the searchlights as it flew over after the bombs had fallen.

The same type of plane had flown twice over Singapore in December a few months ago. One had been shot down on Christmas day itself and a parachute and a few bits of the plane had been displayed in Raffles Hotel in Singapore.

In Singapore in 1941 when I was awakened by the sounds of bombs followed by the wailing of air raid sirens, the sounds of the engines of enemy planes had brought about doubt and fear, of the unknown and of death.

This time, even as the bombs were falling, there arose in me a strange and different feeling. It was not a feeling of fear but of wonderment and a rising sense of exaltation as it became clear that the planes that had come to bomb Bangkok were American planes.

Even as I heard the sounds of bombs whistling by, it was as if I was whistling too. I went outside, not caring about the closeness of the explosions, looking up into the night sky. Perhaps I knew that if I heard the bombs, they would not be meant for me but someone further on helped to assure me.

Everything sounded similar to the bombing of Singapore that signalled the beginning of the war; the searchlights probing the sky, there was the sound of sirens and the closer explosions of the bombs. No doubt the raid would cause similar injuries too.

But my feelings were not the same. The planes were friendly planes, the bombs were friendly bombs and instead of fear, there was elation.

One of the planes suddenly caught in the beam of a searchlight probing the sky began to shine like a silver cigar in the heaven and, immediately, the other searchlights quickly swivelled round to lock on, transfixing it as if on a trestle of beams. It was just like it had taken place in Singapore.

As the beams locked on, the anti-aircraft guns began to bark and when I saw the shells explode like puffs of cotton wool around the plane. This was the only thing that was different. In Singapore the guns had remained silent.

The plane, still looking like a tinsel cigar, slowly drifted away, almost languidly, slowly putting distance between itself and the guns until it slipped away unharmed into the night.

I then knew where my loyalties lay. Everything fell into place. Yamagata was a friend though an enemy, but not in spite of the war. Susumu would always be a friend, war or no war. Japan was a nation at war to which they had loyalty.

But loyalty lay within the definition of nationality, one was or one was not loyal to a nation as a national. One could be loyal to a friend on a personal level. On the personal level, judgement must be based on the individual level and not on a national level. In that way we were friends.

After a while, the guns fell silent and the searchlights, one by one, surrendered to the darkness of the night. Only a B29 could have flown the distance from India or Sri Lanka to Bangkok at that time. But it was a beginning, a beginning to an end.

I saw the others standing beside me but no one passed any comment and I did not feel any different from them. Then, silently, Yamagata, Cho

Suan and I went back indoors and to bed, each with his own thoughts. Where there are conflicting thoughts it would not be strange that such an event would be observed in silence.

The next morning, we got up early and proceeded our quiet way to the rice mill to see if everything was in order. The streets were not crowded and a few fire fighters seemed busy. We saw a few buildings that had been hit but, strangely, saw no one crying.

None of us referred to the bombing, not even Yamagata. I briefly felt sorry for him and then checked myself. This was war and there was no need to be condescending.

We boarded the train feeling somewhat relieved that we were leaving Bangkok. We left with relief, wondering if the planes would return the following night. They did not. But we had been told a lot in that short visit.

When we reached home, we said nothing. We had learnt the lesson that we had to keep our mouths shut too well.

Pak Sako had left an island in Singapore to return to his home. It was significant for him to do that. And more surprising that the Japanese let him do that. The news of what he had done was apparently flashed over the air that he had returned to his *kampung*. That message was supposed to have been a signal that the Malays had now decided that Japan was not to be their ally any longer. Perhaps the situation of the war was already widely accepted for Pak Sako was a great man whose honorary doctorate as a writer was the only tribute to his greatness. Cho Suan is still alive but resting on his laurels in quiet retirement.

*But don't trample the flowers
Nor tread on the tender lilies,
The flowers for the dead. Cover
Those pain wracked faces now at peace
And bury the coffins. Then hope
That war will find another place.*

28. ELECTRA SPEAKS

INDEED, my mosaic of the war is nearly over. The battles had been tough and relentless, also ruthless and sadistic, for that is the nature of war. The innocents had been mowed down with the guilty, for war is single minded. Many would have died unremembered, for war is blind to all but its desire for victory.

In the end, the West, still with the greater power of machines and science, would win and Japan, who had sought to humble others, would be humbled.

Till the very end, the *Kempeitai* kept on moving along in the only way it knew, in a relentless search for those it thought was hostile to Japan although it no longer meant anything since the Japanese empire was tottering and on the brink of collapse, to seek vengeance for its own sake. Till the end, its officers were still looking for victims, trying to do a duty past any use. One of their intended victims was me.

As if in a last spasm, on August 12, 1945, three days before the official surrender of Japan, they came to visit me, hoping to find in me a victim for their brutality.

Two *Kempeitai* Japanese officers in plain clothes came to my tyre retreading premises at the Local Products Company in Maxwell Road. They did not directly tell me why they had come and for a brief moment I thought it was because I had slapped a Japanese soldier on sentry duty outside Fort Auchry at Telok Bahang.

In that incident, I was transporting a Jaguar engine to drive a generator for electricity to electrolyse salt water for the manufacture of caustic soda with which I had hoped to make soap; an experiment which had failed because I could not evaporate enough sea water to have a salinity sufficient enough to electrolyse and a car engine could not generate enough power to obtain any worthwhile result.

Because a permit was required for the transport of engines, I had thought to take the engine round the back of the island to my prawn farm where I could somehow use the engine, even if it was to provide the power for a fast boat to run the south channel.

To do that I had to pass by Fort Auchry which had a Japanese sentry outside its gates the presence of whom I had overlooked.

It was only when I was upon him as I came round the corner with my load and with Seng Hock as my passenger that I suddenly saw him standing on duty with his gun by his side and we were upon the sentry outside Fort Auchry. It was too late but to continue on.

Seeing the car coming round the corner, he stepped into the middle of the road and waved us to a stop. Seng Hock became quite green and he was to tell me that I had become quite white. If the sentry found the engine without a permit, anything could have happened. It was too late to do anything but to pull up.

I was dressed in a white shirt and a pair of white shorts held with a belt. I could pass off as a Japanese if I acted right. By then I had quite a good idea of the psychology of the Japanese soldier.

Notwithstanding what Hatta had said to me about striking a Japanese soldier in uniform, I decided to do just that. It was the only option left to me. As he came up to the car, I opened the door of the car and went up to him and gave him a tight slap across his face and screamed at him. "Buckaroo" and "Coneroo", the two swear words I knew the Japanese officers used. In translation they meant pig and bastard.

He must have been taken aback, for he stepped back sharply, came to attention and bowed smartly and deeply from the waist. Glaring at him, I went back to the vehicle, put it into gear quickly and, still glowering at him, drove quickly past.

If he had asked me any questions at all, I would not have been able to answer him. But, as is often the case of many a feudal mind, he did not think to challenge me and I thought I had escaped again.

Now that the two *Kempeitai* officers had come to the shop, my mind went back to the incident. I wondered if he could have reported the incident and it had been traced to me. I was not driving my car. I had a navy number plate which I had used. He could have noted down that number. But he was an army man and might not have known much about the navy.

Even as I cast my mind around for an excuse, the officers brought about some relief when they began to inquire, not about the incident but about the whereabouts of my lorry which was at that time in Kedah using the navy number plate.

I stalled for a bit. I had a faint idea of what my Chinese-educated manager might have done but it was obvious I could not let on.

I told them that my lorry was at the back of the island making some deliveries and picking up supplies for its return to the city. They hesitated and then they asked me to produce the lorry by the next day when they would turn up to have a look at it.

I could see their game at once. My lorry was in Kedah, to show them I would have to use the cross channel ferry and they would know because every lorry using the ferry had to be checked.

As soon as they had left, I sent someone immediately to Kedah with instructions to remove the lorry from the roads for I knew that it had been used to deliver supplies to the Chinese elements of Force 136 who had asked for cyclostyling paper.

Then I made another set of number plates. It is the practice for imitators of Chinese porcelain to smoke their products, crackle them and soak them in the mud of drainage pits to give them that old look.

I decided to smoke them to turn yellow the fresh white paint and then soak them in the salty mud of Sungei Pinang River to age them. As you know, I had reassembled a few lorries of the same make and had them painted the same colour. My intention was to use one of them which was, in fact, at the back of the island as I had told them, except that it bore a different number.

I sent for the lorry to return at once. The next morning, the lorry had not come and I had to play for time. We also had the general feeling that the war would come to an end soon as Germany had surrendered and the ring round Japan was closing fast.

When they turned up the next morning, I told them they had to return the next day as there was no way I could communicate with the lorry in time—there was, of course, no such telephone service as we know of today.

The next day was August 15, 1945. We did not know that the atom bomb had been dropped. Rumour that the Japanese had surrendered had led to an execution of a Malay who spread the rumour in Singapore. Everyone was silent that morning. We waited, but the Japanese officers did not show up.

Instead of which, Loh Boon Siew, working as a mechanic in the Army workshop at Dato Kramat Road brought in two truck tyres for retreads. He operated a small "mosquito" bus service to Balik Pulau at that time and the retreads were for his buses.

He had a strange question to ask and, looking back, I have a feeling that the retreads were the excuse for him to ask me that question since my father was a lawyer and a judge and he was a very intelligent man. He told me that the three Japanese warehouses in Dato Kramat Road had been deserted by its Japanese sentries and there was no one guarding them. Would it be alright if he went in to help himself to the Koa cigarettes there.

He seemed excited despite his usually controlled expression. He expected an answer and it was a difficult question to answer. He repeated his question and after a while I reminded him that the Japanese had cut off the heads of two youths for looting.

But I added that I was not sure if it would be looting if the godown doors were thrown open to the public as an unspoken invitation for them to help themselves.

He did not think that the British would do that. Unknown to us, Japan had lost the war and the Emperor had surrendered unconditionally to the American forces after the atom bomb had been dropped over Japan. But he must have astutely surmised that the war would soon be over and that the withdrawal of the sentries was an indication of that.

And as he went back to his bicycle to leave us that morning, I had a feeling that he was intelligent enough to know what to do and that he did not expect anything as drastic as had happened to the two youths caught for looting would happen with the British with whose laws we had experienced.

The officers never came that morning nor did they ever turn up. Fate, or luck had once more been in my favour. The war was over.

But Loh Boon Siew turned up again the next day. He had, he said, gone to the godowns that very morning and, though it was still so early in the morning, someone had already opened the doors and people were already helping themselves without any intervention by the Japanese. He had also helped himself to some cigarettes.

He then asked for his tyres and having finished his business with us and placing the tyres behind his bicycle, he went over to the rice stall on the opposite side of the road next to the Prangin Road canal along which the Malay *sampans* used to come to deliver paddy to my grandfather's drying yards and which has now been covered over as a large monsoon drain.

Squatting on the long bench before the rice stall, Chinaman-style, with great calmness and self-control, he began the morning meal he had missed, seemingly oblivious to the fact that an atom bomb had been dropped which had wiped out hundreds of thousands in a holocaust. Everything was so symbolic and he was so in place.

I do not know if Boon Siew had acted with great discretion but he certainly acted with great calmness at that moment of history.

Even as the nuclear clouds of the greatest horror of mankind, the atomic bomb, were drifting away from Nagasaki, Boon Siew, destined to become the richest man in Malaya in his time working single-handedly, was concerned with Koa cigarettes and doing what he was most interested in. The war could look after itself. We were merely the bystanders whom history and the war would ignore.

After telling us he thought the war was over, he rode his bicycle away, the two retreaded tyres slung over both sides of his cycle, held in place by poles slung across the back.

Meanwhile, the quiet wind blew through the streets, rustling the withered leaves alongside the silent drains.

The story is ended, this mosaic of the war is finished. It was as if Electra had spoken and had her revenge. And even as I roll up the screen, I have sadly to say that this may be the end of a war but not all wars. Let us hope I am wrong.

EPILOGUE

*Then, in the midst of this silence,
I thought I saw the Eye looking down
And a voice whispered from the sky—
"And what have you learnt from the war?"*

*I have learnt simple things.
That man is neither good nor bad
But is the result of his nature.*

*For in him lie contradictions
Of opposites, of the good and bad,
Of greed and fear which cause
Selfishness and cowardice and
Acts of viciousness, cruelty and sadism;
Courage and generosity
That bring nobility and kindness;
And such other opposites that make up
His nature, personality and character.*

*It is dependent on which predominate
That make him good or bad. Some
Are born to goodness, some to evil made.
They do what their nature makes them do.*

*For the welfare of all, he must
By discipline and law be controlled.*

*I now know that war comes when ambition,
And overbearing arrogance and righteousness
Dismiss the balance that make for sanity
And poke a finger into the face of law.*

Rationalisation and self-aggrandisement
Become the rule and justification,
The excuses for murder and rape.

In the name of their beliefs,
They justify their acts of cruelty
As the punishment of evil and
Destruction as acts of holy sacrifice.
Self-righteousness makes the betrayals
Of friends honourable things and
Selfishness, bigotry, vanity and greed
The natural acts of human beings.

I have heard of the deeds of Genghis Khan,
Of Tamerlane the Great; of the deeds
Of great men of history such as Alexander,
Of Napoleon and of Hitler,
Who have tried to make great nations
After their own image to last forever.

I have also heard of men who built
Great cities like Samarkand and Constantinople
Edifices such as the Taj Mahal,
Material monuments of great and wondrous beauty
That have died or lie dying in the sun.
Men in history have done great acts
But I now know they did what they did,
Not because they were believed but because
Their ambitious natures told them so.

Thus have they also distorted the truth,
Blinded themselves in their own beliefs,
Committed the most heinous of crimes as well,
Because their very natures have compelled it so.

So I think no more of greatness
Or to build such magnificence as

*Flatter the ego of men or add to
Vainness and the pomp and ceremony of men;
But in more noble and cultural things
That will ennoble the human mind,
Enrich our cultures and make us turn from war.*

*So also have I dreamt of enrichment
Without war and in peace, wherein
I still can see such as the mighty caravans
Of ancient Samarkand plod the silk road,
Arab seafarers and Ming vessels
Traverse the seas to enrich
The cultures of different nations.*

*I also dream great dreams of hope,
Have visions of the mighty fortresses of faith
Where men speak in modesty and gentleness
And extend to others what he extends to himself.*

*I can see there is no continental divide
But an East and a West blessed as one,
Not in fear by isolation bred.*

*In that world I can also see such men
Of such nature as would incline to goodness.
But as nations do mirror the nature of leaders,
It becomes a danger when evil men rule
Or when their sanity is disturbed
As the elements of evil outbalance their opposites.*

*So, as with nations, shall it be with men.
If we are to stop the hideous cycles
Of war and peace, there shall be such
International institutions as the ill-fated League
Or the creaky United Nations but with laws
Such as are beyond the will of individual nations
And their recalcitrant leaders.*

BLOOD ON THE GOLDEN SANDS

And in my dreams I still see the mountains
Where still the aspen trees grow
And there are clean lichen and mosses
Amidst the creeks and mountain springs.

I know that it is a dream I see.
But then, what distinguishes a man
But his faith and hope and his dreams.

Let us search for those springs.
For, we must not forget that beauty grows
Not only from the mud and filth,
But also in innocence and virgin lands.

Lim Kean Siew

Born in 1922, Lim Kean Siew comes from one of Malaysia's most distinguished families. Educated at Raffles College in Singapore before World War II, he went to Cambridge where he obtained a double Tripos in English and Law, and went on to follow in his father's footsteps, a well-known advocate who served on the Legislative Council in colonial times, to become a barrister-at-law at Gray's Inn.

Lim's interest in law and literature stems from his lifelong love of poetry and philosophy. An accomplished photographer, writer and poet, he studied philosophy while at Cambridge, though he never took a degree in it.

On returning to Malaysia after a short stint in London, he was admitted as an advocate in the Malaysian Bar, went into politics and became a leader of the Labour Party, the Socialist Front and the Socialist Conference, holding many positions, including that of secretary-general in all three organisations. Malaysia was then moving towards Independence. He joined the Labour Party and became an MP and leader of the Opposition, and years later, a senator. Because of his Buddhist beliefs, he declined a ministerial post in 1960 and that of a judge of the appellate court in 1965, a year of political turmoil, which saw the breakaway of Singapore from Malaysia. Although he was then the secretary-general of the Socialist Front, he was offered the post of leader of the Malaysian branch of the People's Action Party, a post which he declined. That was before Singapore separated from the Federation of Malaysia.

In 1975, he was approached to join the Malaysian Chinese Association when the Socialist Front and the Labour Party went defunct. On a promise that his views on equality for all races would be accepted, he joined the MCA as a presidential adviser and became a member of the Presidential Council and Central Committee. Unfortunately, his blueprint for basic equality was never fulfilled for Dato' Lee San Choon suddenly, though not surprisingly, resigned from the presidency in 1983.

Lim resigned from the MCA and all political positions in 1983, and is now a legal adviser for the Malaysian Buddhist Association Meditation Centre in Penang.

Lim is the author of *The Eye Over the Golden Sands* and *Inner Peace: A Source of Chinese Philosophic Meditative Practice*.

ALSO BY LIM KEAN SIEW

INNER PEACE
A Source of Chinese Philosophic Meditative Practice
LIM KEAN SIEW   ISBN 967 978 474 6   PELANDUK PUBLICATIONS

THIS book attempts to remove some of the misunderstandings that have grown like cobwebs throughout the ages to cloud the true nature of meditation caused by indifferent explanations, superstitions and mysteries surrounding the subject due to the use of animal symbolism and animism to explain abstract and philosophical thoughts to primitive peoples.

Meditation must be experienced to be understood. It is the power of the mind over matter. Though it has remained an unresolved mystery, one thing is for certain—the mind has powers over illnesses; it reduces stress, improves heart conditions, or simply induces relaxation. There is in every one of us the ability to attain genuine inner peace amidst the stress of modern living through meditation.

Through meditation, you can gain the confidence to achieve a fuller, richer life. You will not only enjoy important mental and spiritual experiences, but also find that powerful therapeutic forces have been set at work in your life to change your view of yourself and your concept of the universe of which you are a part, all towards discovering the self you never knew existed.

THE EYE OVER THE GOLDEN SANDS
LIM KEAN SIEW   ISBN 967 978 567 x   PELANDUK PUBLICATIONS

THIS autobiography chronicles the life and times of an affluent Straits Chinese trading family in Penang, part of a unique community in the social fabric of Malaya, at the beginning of the tail-end of the British Empire, just before World War I and ending with the advent of World War II and the Japanese Occupation. It weaves not only a rich tapestry of characters and conflicts within a family, but also a memorable, detailed picture of a society that dictated that life. Set against a period of British colonialism and a world in transition, it draws you into a life, a culture and a colourful period in Malayan history. By delving into the fascinating life of an English-educated Asian family against the history of Penang and its people—a society caught in the turmoil of change and progress—we are made to realise that people are moulded by their environment, education and parentage.